WESTERN
PLEASURE
Training and Showing to Win

DOUG CARPENTER
with Carolyn S. Pryor

WESTERN PLEASURE
Training and Showing to Win

DOUG CARPENTER
with Carolyn S. Pryor

published by
EQUIMEDIA

WESTERN
PLEASURE
Training and Showing to Win

Doug Carpenter *Author*
Carolyn S. Pryor *Editor*
  Photographer
Robert Feinberg *Graphic Designer*
  Illustrator
Taro Kodama *Production Asst.*

Library of Congress Cataloging-in-Publication Data
Carpenter, Doug, 1956-
    Western Pleasure : training and showing to win / Doug Carpenter with Carolyn S. Pryor. -- 1st ed.
        190 p.: col. ill.; 29 cm. -- (EquiMedia's masters series)
    Includes index.
    ISBN 0-9625898-3-7 : $29.95
    1. Western show horses--Training.   2. Horse shows--Western division and classes. I. Pryor, Carolyn S.   II. Title. III. Series.
SF296.W47 C38 1995   96-136022
                                                          CIP

Published by
EquiMedia Corporation
P.O. Box 90519
Austin, TX 78709
Tel: 512-288-1676

Printed in China
10 9 8 7 6 5 4 3
00 99 98 97

*I dedicate this book
to the memory of Rodney Miller
for sharing with me an appreciation for a good horse
and the desire to always be the best in the arena.
Good friends are never forgotten.*

Contents

Preface

BY CAROLYN S. PRYOR

If you own, breed or ride a western pleasure horse, you've probably been asked what this event is all about. Most often the questions come from people who have never seen the class. From my own experience, it seems there's not an easy answer to this question because in order to define western pleasure you have to explain more than just the class requirements.

In this book, Doug Carpenter gives us the entire story. His dedication to the event becomes an encyclopedia for understanding western pleasure. Both the words and the photographs provide a thorough comprehension of, as well as an appreciation for, western pleasure. The real beauty in it however, is Doug's straightforward, black and white approach to training. For example, I remember one of our interview sessions when I kept asking Doug what the rider should be doing to push each part of the horse's body into a specific position at the lope. He finally just told me, it isn't that complicated. He said you have to begin with a horse who can lope naturally and then you merely teach him to hold that position. Replacing the horse's natural ability with a man-made way of moving is not what western pleasure is all about.

In writing this book with Doug, I learned that it doesn't take a lot of fancy theories or complicated training methods to make a nice horse. It does require a great deal of time and patience as well as a good, solid understanding of what western pleasure is all about. Obviously the former is up to the you as the reader, but understanding the event can be accomplished by reading the information Doug provides on the following pages. I think you'll find the book both interesting and enjoyable to read whether you actually ride pleasure horses or simply admire them from afar, and perhaps the next time anyone else asks "what is western pleasure," you can simply hand them the book.

Profile

Raised in a middle class suburban neighborhood with small backyards and busy paved roads, Doug Carpenter considers himself lucky to be a horseman. Not only did he find a lucrative career in the equine industry, he also thinks his childhood association with horses probably kept him out of the kind of trouble accessible to any bored youngster in the city.

Doug was born in 1956 in Cumberland, Rhode Island. His father Jesse, now deceased, was a policeman, and his mother Jacqueline was a housewife raising Doug, his sister and brother. The family's introduction to horses came from family friends who competed at open shows.

"There wasn't much for us kids to do in the summers or after school. We liked the horses because it gave us a family activity," Doug explains. When he was twelve-years-old, each of the Carpenters pooled their money and purchased a sorrel mare named Ginger for two hundred and fifty dollars. Doug's share was thirty-five dollars, earned by mowing lawns and doing odd jobs. They kept the mare at their grandfather's barn which was about a mile away from home.

"That first horse taught me a lot of responsibility. An animal like that takes a lot of work and that kept me out of trouble. Looking back, I really think I might have taken a wrong turn in life if it hadn't been for that horse and the positive influence it provided," Doug says. Rather than hanging out on street corners with other boys his age, Doug was busy at the barn — cleaning stalls, feeding, grooming and riding seven days a week. Soon most of his friends were horse show people, and horses became a way of life for Doug.

Eventually the rest of the family lost interest in riding, but Doug's friendship with local horseman Bob Schofield gave Doug a glimpse of the larger horse shows and spurred his interest. With Schofield's encouragement, Doug began to discover a talent and a love for riding. He was fascinated by the idea of showing horses, but believed he'd never be able to afford the type of horse it took to compete at the registered Quarter Horse shows.

"Going to those local Quarter Horse shows in the New England area with Bob, I met another trainer named Jack Farrell. I didn't have a horse to show, but I'd help other people, like Jack, prepare their horses. I guess I was about in the eighth grade when Jack invited me to a clinic he was putting on that summer. Jack told me he thought I had a lot of ability, and I could really learn a lot there. I wanted to go, but it cost two hundred dollars for five days, and I knew there was no way I could come up

When Doug was 12 years old, his family pooled their money and bought this mare named Ginger.

with that kind of money. I told him I appreciated it, but I wasn't interested in coming.

"The next weekend I saw Jack again, and he was persistent about me coming to that clinic. Finally I told him I just didn't have the money. He looked at me for a long time and then he said, `Well, just come on anyway. Forget the money.' That was a big thrill for me because I really wanted to go. It's one of those things you don't ever forget."

Doug went to the clinic and worked to pay his way by cleaning stalls and helping out with daily chores. He ended up staying at Jack Farrel's ranch in Durham, Connecticut, for an additional two weeks after the clinic, and over the next few years he spent entire summers working for and learning from Farrell.

"Like everybody in those days, we were riding all around horses. The events weren't segregated like they are today. I enjoyed anything that had to do with riding, but the halter just didn't thrill me at all. Jack gave me a horse or two to show, but mainly I was just riding and breaking colts."

After graduating from high school in 1974, Doug moved to Newark, Ohio, to run a small breeding farm there. At the time, he was also offered a job by noted trainer Tommy Manion but passed on that opportunity for vague reasons Doug later regretted. He spent the next two years working in Ohio and trying to get another chance to ride for Manion.

It was March of 1978 before an opening came up at Manion's. This time Doug didn't miss his opportunity. Having just turned 22 with a full beard and long hair, he quit his job in Ohio and drove all night to get to Manion's barn in Springfield, Illinois. He spent his last dime on breakfast and was waiting in his truck when Manion arrived at the barn at eight that morning. Manion quickly evaluated Doug's abilities and put him to work riding the outstanding string of horses he had at that time.

Doug acknowledges that his good fortune was accentuated by both great horses and Manion's goals. "Tommy was looking for somebody to do the riding at home which would free him up to travel and do other things. What he did, which was to my benefit, was to let me ride those really good horses. He'd ride a horse at home first, and when he got that horse going like he wanted it to go at the horse show, he'd bring it right over to me. He'd make me ride so I could feel it, and he'd say `this is how I want them to go. That's how I got the feel down. He could have told me about it all day long, but it was only when I actually felt the difference that it started connecting with me on how to make these horses operate at the level he competed on."

Doug started showing horses for Manion that first year. At his first trip to the All American Quarter Horse Congress, Doug placed second out of more than 300 entries in the Two-Year-Old Pleasure Futurity on Good Lookin Babe, and Manion finished third. Doug's share of

Harold Campton

the $10,000 paid for reserve marked the first time he won any money. "I didn't necessarily get a big charge out of finishing second, but I had fun. That mare was very green when Tommy gave her to me to ride in June, and I had to really work to catch up. It was personally rewarding that I got the horse that was started late and made her work.

"The whole experience was influential to my career. Just seeing the magnitude of that show and watching all the other trainers and horses from across the country, I realized how much I liked the atmosphere there. It was exciting, and I knew I wanted to be there every year."

After working for Manion from 1978 through 1980, Doug was ready for a change. At the time, he had a two-year-old mare named Miss Docs Melody on his string of horses, and at the owner's request and with Manion's blessings, Doug took the mare with him when he left Manion's to start his own training operation in Pilot Point, Texas. Getting that mare proved to be influential to Doug's career not only because of the success that followed, but also for the lessons learned along the way.

Doug showed at the All American Quarter Horse Congress for the first time in 1978. He placed second out of more than 300 entries in the Two-Year-Old Pleasure Futurity on Good Lookin Babe.

13

Since he didn't start riding Miss Docs Melody until midway through her two-year-old, she wasn't shown until she was a three-year-old. Both he and owner Karen Sullivan qualified the mare for the AQHA World Championship Show in the Open and Amateur pleasures that year, and they took her to Oklahoma City where Sullivan started things off by winning the World Championship in Amateur Western Pleasure.

"Despite Karen's win, I went into the Junior Pleasure with a negative attitude because I showed the mare at the Congress and had a good ride, but got over-looked," he says. His lack of enthusiasm was obvious as Doug rode in the first go-round in a work shirt without a tie, but after winning that go by unanimous decision he says his spirits brightened and his attitude improved.

"On the night of the finals I was warming up my mare when she spooked from a horse wearing a blue cooler who was tied to the rail outside the pen. Right away I knew my mare was too fresh. With twenty minutes until the class began, I took her outside by herself and loped her down. When we went in the class, she was probably still a little too fresh, but she showed well and we won it."

Winning that World Championship meant more to Doug than a trophy and a buckle. "It was a turning point in my career because it made me want to get serious about riding horses. I had been discouraged because I wasn't winning much, and I felt I could never make it in the business. I enjoyed the horses, but until that night I think I could have just as soon gone off and drove a bull-dozer for a living."

In 1984, Doug accepted an offer to work for John Mulholland in Edmond, Oklahoma. Mulholland had a good eye for buying horses, Doug prepared them and the pair resold them. It was at a horse show in Oklahoma that Doug met Tammy Eddie of Oklahoma City who showed with trainer Dale Livingston. Doug and Tammy married in 1986.

The following year brought another significant change for Doug. After a job interview that brought him to Memphis failed to work out, his love for the land in that area and its central location prompted him and Tammy to move to Hernando in northern Mississippi. They bought a log cabin on 13 acres and built a barn.

At about the same time, a friend and fellow horse-man, Keith Whistle, was leaving his position at a nearby farm. "It was kind of like neither one of us had anywhere else to be so we ended up working together," Doug explains. The pair launched a successful program which primarily revolved around Doug's training talents and Whistle's showmanship abilities. Together they have won every major pleasure futurity and have produced numerous Congress winners and World Champions.

"I've always been self-motivated, but things are never easy for me," Doug explains regarding his success in the pleasure horse industry. "Unlike a lot of horse trainers, I wasn't born on a ranch and my father wasn't a horse trainer. I don't even think I had a lot of natural talent. I started out teaching myself, so naturally I made a lot of mistakes and picked up bad habits which are hard to break."

"But once I set my mind on doing things, I have a determination which seems to win out in the end. Certain people made a real difference in my career and in my life, but it's probably the horses who made me the person I am today. As a kid, owning a horse gave me a purpose. It wasn't like playing a sport, where you could always forget about it for a few days. The horse required my time and attention every single day. And now it's a job which requires the same.

"Taking care of an animal or animals really teaches you about responsibility. Training and showing the horse also gives a child or a person self-esteem and self-worth. It is demanding, but it's also rewarding."

Today the walls of the Carpenter home are filled with trophies and belt buckles from Doug's professional success as well as wild game souvenirs from his personal love for hunting and the outdoors. Doug and Tammy have two daughters, Katelyn and Kelly.

Introduction

BY DOUG CARPENTER

I enjoy riding any kind of horse, but there's something about a western pleasure horse that has always intrigued me. I think it's because western pleasure is all about working hard to make something look easy. It begins by taking a horse's potential, no matter what age or how talented that particular individual might be, and using my mind and riding skills to shape and mold the potential into a broke horse.

The end result has to be a horse that walks, jogs and lopes to the best of his ability while performing in a horse show environment. Control is critical. I may have the best loper in the pen, but the horse is judged to be a pleasure to ride only if he lopes well with little assistance from the rider. My job as the trainer is to prepare that horse so that everything he does appears effortless. It's the challenge of creating that final product of a nice, well-broke horse that motivates and inspires me each day.

Experience has taught me that the more broke the horse is, the better my chances are of winning. I have always been extremely competitive and very determined to be the best in whatever I do, so I put a lot of thought as well as many hours in the saddle in attempting to create winning pleasure horses. This book is intended to help you create a horse that is a pleasure to ride. Whether you own a horse just for fun or you are competitive at any level, I hope the techniques and advice provided on the following pages will prove as rewarding for you as my experience with pleasure horses is for me.

1

Evolution of the Western Pleasure Horse

Western pleasure was born when people began looking for a western style horse that was smooth and easy to ride. Some people argue it originated out on the range, when horsemen decided they wanted a comfortable ride out of a horse that they previously only expected to be durable and dependable. But for our purposes, western pleasure originated when that search for a pleasurable ride turned into a judged competition, i.e., when one man's opinion of the horses in an arena determined which horses were best-suited for riding purely for enjoyment.

The American Quarter Horse Association approved western pleasure as an official event in 1959. Initial rules and definitions in the AQHA handbook were vague at best, describing the class as "Open to registered Quarter Horses...normally used for pleasure to be shown at a walk, trot and lope on a reasonably loose rein without undue restraint. Entries shall be penalized for being on wrong lead at a lope." No further description of movement was provided, however it was stated that the class would be judged 60 percent on performance, 30 percent on conformation and 10 percent on appointments.

Appointments were defined with the following: "Horses shall be shown with a stock saddle, but silver equipment will not count over a good working outfit. A hackamore or a curb, half-breed or spade bit is permissible but a martingale or tie-down is prohibited. When a horse is shown with a bit, a bosal is permitted, provided two fingers can be placed between bosal and horse's chin. No wire curbs, regardless of how padded or taped, or no chin strap narrower than one-half inch will be permitted. Chain curbs are permissible but must be of the standard flat variety with no twist and must meet the

The first AQHA Honor Roll Western Pleasure horse was Mohawk Buck, a nine-year-old buckskin gelding owned by Alan Potts of Coshocton, Ohio.

(pages 18-19) By the early 1980's, when Doug showed Smokeys Grey, western pleasure horses were the product of both the California style of riding and the more western look of the traditional cowboy's horse.

approval of the judge." The only other requirements were that the riders must wear a Western hat and cowboy boots, that shoes other than standard horseshoes were to be discouraged and that reins must be held in one hand and could not be changed during performance.

With no further specifications or any tangible guidance such as a timer or pattern with required maneuvers, judges based their decisions strictly on how enjoyable the ride appeared to be for the person on the horse's back. They looked for the horse that wasn't a struggle to ride; one that responded to fairly subtle cues and had a relaxed, easy-going nature which meant the rider didn't have to struggle to keep the horse under control and traveling at a relaxed pace. A good pleasure horse also appeared to give a smooth ride, as opposed to a rough or jarring one.

That first year the high point western pleasure horse in the nation was Mohawk Buck, a nine-year-old buckskin gelding by Yellow Buck. Owned by Allan Potts of Coshocton, Ohio, Mohawk Buck won the high point title with 15 points. Mohawk Buck also had points and or high point titles in trail, working cow horse and reining and was an AQHA champion.

Back when I started showing horses as a kid, everybody got their horses broke for western pleasure. A person would start out doing the halter when the horse was a weanling and a yearling and then break the horse for western pleasure. After that, he'd find out what other events the horse was capable of doing, like roping, reining or cutting. But every horse was broke for western pleasure. It was a starter class, and usually if a horse didn't pass the western pleasure that horse wasn't good enough to show in anything else either.

By the late 1970s, the western pleasure class became popular in its own right rather than just as a starter class for other events. This was largely due to the formation of AQHA's Amateur division in 1979. Amateur Western Pleasure was a good class for non-professionals because they didn't have to match up with a cow or follow a complicated pattern while riding fast. They could just enjoy riding a horse competitively in a relatively relaxed atmosphere.

By this time exhibitors also began refining certain aspects of the way their pleasure horses rode. Brokeness became critical as we trained the horses to respond to cues which were virtually invisible to the judge, and we started expecting the pleasure horse to walk, jog and lope at a slightly slower pace. There was a lot of talk about collection and drive from behind, and we became much more advanced in our training techniques. Horsemen on the West Coast developed a new look in which the horse's nose was tucked so that his face was practically perpendicular to the ground. This new bridled look, which came to be called the "California style," was very different from the more casual, relaxed look of the horses throughout the rest of the country. Yet people were intrigued by the California style because a horse appeared to be more broke if he relaxed his neck just a little bit and tucked his nose in toward his chest.

Before long many trainers, particularly those on the West Coast, further increased the degree of difficulty by training the horses to carry their heads in this new position and move slowly while on a loose rein. Everything revolved around making the horse look easy to ride. The new trend really took off when a few horses came along that had the natural ability to move much slower with their noses tucked in, yet on a loose rein, and they won. Horses like Physical Ed, the World Champion in Senior Western Pleasure in 1977 and 1978 with Kenny Eppers, inspired many of us to train our horses to have this new look rather than just going around the pen with no particular style.

By the early 1980s the new bridled look of the horses on the West Coast seemed to merge with the very natural, western look of the horses typical in Texas, and the industry found a happy medium. The horses weren't quite as bridled as they had been on the West Coast, but they still had a lot of collection and drive from behind. They also moved a good bit slower than in year's past.

In 1979 Doug showed Prissy Mistress at the All American Quarter Horse Congress.

In 1984 Doug finished second in the Congress Two-Year-Old Pleasure Futurity on Ms MBJ Mudlark and Jody Galyean won the event on Mr Zippo Pine. Both horses are now considered to be two of the greatest horses in pleasure horse history.

Horses like Bonanzas Rosy and Bonanzas Rosy Two, full-sisters shown by Jody Galyean to Congress wins in 1981, exemplified the kind of horse we were all striving to produce through both new breeding programs and our training techniques.

It was also during this period that the concept of the western pleasure futurity became enormously popular. First with the Congress and then the Texas Classic and Texas Breeders' Futurity, the two-year-old pleasure futurities gave people an incentive to show younger horses. It was an exciting and enthusiastic period in the pleasure horse industry.

The popularity of the western pleasure futurities inspired the formation of the National Snaffle Bit Association in 1983. According to the association's handbook, the purpose of the NSBA is "to define, promote and improve the quality of the snaffle bit working horse; to promote exhibits, events and contests in expositions and shows; to promote the training of snaffle bit horses, to promote interest in snaffle bit horses among the younger horsemen and to use and encourage the use of the standard rules for holding and judging contests of the snaffle bit horse." With time, the term "snaffle bit horse" came to include all western pleasure horses as well as hunter under saddle horses.

With a membership made up of pleasure horse owners, breeders and trainers, NSBA set most of the standards by which horses are judged in all pleasure futurities. The association provides specific descriptions of each gait, equipment regulations, penalties for faults and other rules which are outlined in the NSBA handbook.

Since it's inception in 1983, NSBA went through several phases, including tremendous membership support in its earliest years and a period of decline in the late 1980s. But since 1991, the association experienced phenomenal growth which seems to reflect a renewed interest in western pleasure and hunter under saddle futurity events as well as a confidence in the pleasure horse industry in general.

AQHA has also weathered storms surrounding western pleasure. Controversy regarding low head carriage and what many perceived to be excessive slowness prompted the association to make new rules beginning in 1993 which specify low head carriage, overflexing at the poll, and excessive slowness or loss of forward momentum as faults to be scored according to severity or even cause for disqualification in some instances. These new AQHA rules, along with the industry's general attitude that it was time to rely on the pleasure horse's inherent ability rather than trying to forcibly train these skills into a horse, led to a return to the more natural way of going. According to Cam Foreman, AQHA Senior Director of Judges and Shows, "Over the past few years much time and effort have been devoted to the western pleasure class to make sure the horses are shown in accordance with AQHA rules. I am very pleased with how the owners and exhibitors have made changes with their horses to make sure they are in compliance with the rules. With the changes that have occurred, I believe the western pleasure class has a bright future."

In many ways the evolution of the western pleasure horse has brought the class back closer to its roots than ever before. Judging is never an exact science, but most people within the industry want to see a pleasure horse carry his head in a completely natural, comfortable position in relation to his conformation. They want the horse's legs moving freely to produce the mandatory beats with each gait. Last but not least, everyone within the industry wants to see that the horse is healthy and happy with his job. All of this contributes to making the horse a pleasure to ride.

The primary difference between the horses of today and the horses back when the western pleasure class was invented is the degree of difficulty which has naturally risen as the event evolved. In the 1960s the horses shown in western pleasure were bred to be all around athletes. They were shorter and heavier built with more energetic dispositions. They could compete in a halter class, cut a cow, run a reining pattern and then go around the rail for the pleasure class. Today, after establishing a few generations of pleasure horse bloodlines, the horses are physically and mentally inclined to do primarily one thing — western pleasure. Chapter Two: Breeding for Pleasure Horses and Chapter 3: Selecting the Pleasure Prospect cover this in greater detail, however for the purpose of understanding how the industry evolved it's important to note that we are now at a point where breeding has made a difference in our industry's standards. To put it simply, we can now say we want a natural pleasure horse because western pleasure now comes naturally to many horses.

As any sport evolves, it becomes more competitive. Race cars go faster today than they did ten years ago. More basketball players can now slam dunk the ball than when the NBA was formed. And western pleasure horses are now bred and trained to walk, jog and lope with greater finesse than back when the horse who got both leads was called out as the winner. It's an ever-changing process, but I think that we learn from the past as we continue to improve our training programs, to define our objectives in the show pen, and ultimately, to ride better pleasure horses.

2

Breeding for Pleasure Horses

As the pleasure horse industry evolves, we determine more and more about the kind of horses we want to ride. We define the conformation, athletic talent and mental capacity that sets the pleasure horse apart from a cutting horse or a halter horse or any other horse bred for a specific purpose. And as we decide not only what makes them different, we also determine what makes one pleasure horse superior to another. We're discovering the importance of breeding.

The pleasure horse industry didn't really begin breeding for pleasure horses until the late 1970's and the early 1980's. Before then, we either rode horses who were rejected for halter competition or those all around horses who were more inclined to jog and lope smoothly than they were to catch a cow or swap a lead. There really were no pleasure horse sires.

It was around 1977 that a young red roan stallion named Speedy Glow developed a reputation for producing horses who were good movers and were also easy to break and ride. Speedy Glow was sired by Poco Red Bar who is by Three Bars (TB). Speedy Glow was out of a Poco Bueno mare named O's Linda Lee. According to Shorty Parks, trainer and breeding manager for Kenneth Grantham who owned Speedy Glow from 1974 through 1977, "We mostly got little, ol' cheap mares to breed back in those days, but Speedy Glow helped them all. His colts had straight legs and good minds, but most importantly they looked completely different through the head, neck, shoulder and even the tail. Their necks came straight out from their shoulders so they had a flatter topline; they carried their heads with their faces more straight up and down as opposed to having their noses pushed out like

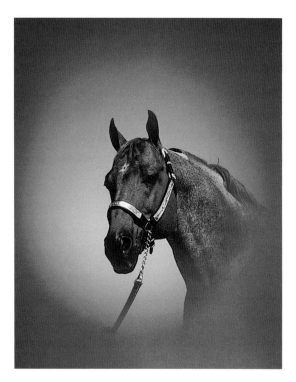

the horses from earlier years; and they carried their tails flat which created a totally new look."

Speedy Glow's early offspring included such winning pleasure horses as Old Glow Pal who won the All American Quarter Horse Congress Pleasure Futurity in 1972 and was the AQHA high point junior western pleasure horse in 1973. There were other sires around that time who produced good pleasure horses, yet they were just as well known for producing halter or performance horses. But when someone mentioned Speedy Glow, you knew they were talking strictly about pleasure horses. I consider Speedy Glow to be the first pleasure horse sire.

As the industry grew in popularity, a demand for pleasure horses was created and people naturally wanted to raise them. At this point I don't think most breeders knew exactly what crosses created an inherently good pleasure horse, but as we bred more and more of them we found out what worked and what did not.

In 1980, The Invester became the hot horse in pleasure horse circles. That year in the Congress Pleasure Futurity, the top four two-year-olds were all sired by The Invester. The Invester is out of the first colt crop of Zippo

Pat Bars, a son of Three Bars (TB). The dam of Zippo Pat Bars was Leo Pat by Leo. The dam of The Invester is Hank's Peppy Lou who traces to the legendary Joe Reed.

In The Invester's offspring we saw several common physical characteristics which made them good pleasure horses including strong backs and low hocks. Those conformation traits are now considered to be among the pleasure horse's most important structural qualities, and I believe The Invester is largely responsible for helping us recognize their significance.

In the mid-eighties the National Snaffle Bit Association was formed and the notion of showing young pleasure horses in snaffle bits helped lead to the popu-

(pages 24-25) With each generation we discover more and more about the importance of breeding in the pleasure horse industry.

(opposite top) Speedy Glow, by Poco Red Bar, is believed to be the first pleasure horse sire.

(opposite bottom) The Invester, by Zippo Pat Bars, is known for putting strong backs and low hocks on his offspring.

(below) Zippo Pine Bar, by Zippo Pat Bars and out of Dollie Pine by Poco Bueno, is the most famous pleasure horse sire in NSBA, Quarter Horse, Appaloosa, Paint and Palomino competition.

Peri

larity of a stallion whose get excelled in this milder equipment. Not only did Zippo Pine Bar become known as a pleasure horse sire, he came to be considered the pleasure horse sire. Zippo Pine Bar, a half-brother to The Invester and also from Zippo Pat Bars first colt crop, is out of Dollie Pine who goes back to Poco Bueno who is by King P-234.

Known throughout the horse industry as "the Zippos," the offspring of Zippo Pine Bar dominated every major pleasure horse event in NSBA, Quarter Horse, Appaloosa, Paint and Palomino competition in the late 1980's and continue to do so through the time of publication of this book. His son, Zips Chocolate Chip, has also become a renowned pleasure horse sire. Zippo Pine Bar's contributions to the pleasure horse industry are many, but he is most often credited for passing along a trademark laid-back attitude. This idea of being great-minded, is now practically part of the definition of the term "pleasure horse."

Two other sires have contributed significantly to the evolution of the modern pleasure horse, Hotrodders Jet Set and Barpasser. Hotrodders Jet Set, a bay stallion whose career as a leading pleasure hose sire ended tragically with his death in May of 1992, achieved both fame and respect in just eight years as a breeding horse. The bay stallion was sired by Docs Hotrodder who was by Doc Bar. Hotrodders Jet Set's dam, Miss Clique, was a double-bred Leo mare.

Hotrodders Jet Set was an extremely athletic horse, and was recognized as having a lot of balance and great strength across the top of his body. He passed these qualities on to his get, and their achievements at the major shows and futurities proved Hotrodders Jet Set's impact on the industry.

Barpasser was sired by Senior Bardeck, who was by a full-brother to Jet Deck, and was out of a granddaughter of Sugar Bars named Ranch Bars Vandy. Barpasser had an exceptionally level topline which probably put him fifteen years ahead of his time back when he was being shown in the late seventies and early eighties. Those horsemen who saw Barpasser back in those days, had a glimpse of the future and most geared their breeding and training programs toward imitating Barpasser's unique look. Equally important to the evolution of the industry, Barpasser produced several great horses who also became top pleasure horse sires including Ima Big Leaguer and Barpassers Image.

There are several other stallions who have produced nice pleasure horses, however I consider these to be the main pleasure horse sires. Each made significant contributions to the evolution of the modern pleasure horse. Note that they all go back to Three Bars (TB) on the top side and all but Barpasser are out of King bred mares. Barpasser's dam traces back to Three Bars (TB).

No discussion on bloodlines or breeding would be complete without mentioning the importance of the mare. As Bob Loomis wrote in *Reining, The Art of Performance in Horses*, "In order for a stallion to sire well, he must be crossed on good mares. However, it is equally important that he have an outstanding mare for a mother." All of the truly great pleasure horses prove this theory to be true.

As I state in Chapter 4 on Selecting the Pleasure Prospect, the dam's show or produce records tell me a lot about her foals. If she was successful as a show horse, I know she has what it takes. If she has already produced foals who are point or money earners, I also know she can pass on that inherent ability. I like riding a horse who has a good dam, and I'm always more likely to buy a horse when I know he or she has a good mother.

The pleasure horse business is young enough that our breeding programs are still changing as we discover what crosses work well and which ones don't. One theory I hope we have learned is the importance of breeding like to like. Horsemen such as myself came to recognize this following a trend in the early 1980's when many owners bred their great pleasure horse mares to halter horse sires hoping to get pretty pleasure horses. What they usually ended up with were horses who couldn't compete in pleasure or halter. That trend created a market where there were very few really good pleasure horses.

Today we recognize the significance of breeding in our horses. We know that we need balanced athletes with reasonably quiet temperments. We see that the great movers come from specific lines, and that certain crosses produce conformation traits desirable in our pleasure horses. Through better breeding, we're creating a better pleasure horse.

3

Selecting the Pleasure Prospect

I pick out a prospect for western pleasure by looking for the basic physical and mental qualities necessary in an outstanding, finished pleasure horse. Since I do not raise my own pleasure prospects, the young horses I ride are usually ones I purchase for myself or my clients. My advice in this chapter on purchasing a prospect is also applicable in evaluating horses you raise or already own.

Without getting into which particular bloodlines I personally prefer, I strongly suggest choosing a prospect who is bred to be a pleasure horse. This is a relatively new concept within this industry. In year's past, we just evaluated a horse we were considering buying by his individual talents and characteristics. It was considered a plus if a horse we liked also happened to be well-bred, but specific bloodlines weren't mandatory. For many years the horses shown in western pleasure were either all around horses or horses who didn't succeed in halter or a performance event like reining or roping. Today, horses are bred specifically for western pleasure so good breeding is important, particularly for resale value. When I look at a prospect, I ask about the sire's and dam's show or produce records. If neither accomplished anything as a pleasure horse or has ever produced a pleasure horse, I don't expect the offspring will be the caliber of horse I'm looking for.

Most people buy pleasure horse prospects either in the fall of their yearling year or as green-broke two-year-olds the following spring. Whatever age the horse might be, two things influence me as to whether I buy a prospect: my first impression of their overall "look" or physical appearance and their talents as a mover. There are certain qualities and characteristics that I like in a

(pages 30-31) The first thing Doug looks at when inspecting a pleasure prospect is the face.

horse's structure, but most are so obvious that I see them upon first glance. After that, I'm concerned only with soundness and ability.

FIRST IMPRESSIONS

I am a firm believer in first impressions, mainly because I think they strongly influence a judge as he places the horses in a class. Therefore, before beginning a critical evaluation of a prospect's talents, I first spend a few minutes glancing over a prospect and forming an initial opinion of his physical characteristics. This may take place in the horse's stall, in the hallway of the barn or, with yearlings, out in the pasture. I concentrate on three specific things; the horse's face, his profile from the withers forward, and a profile of his back and everything which will extend behind the saddle. I make my observations in this specific order because it is basically the same order in which a judge sees that horse as it enters the arena for competition. Finally, I put all the parts together and look for balance.

Checking for soundness is part of the entire process, but at this stage it is not my primary concern. I wait to make a close inspection of the horse's feet and legs until after seeing the horse move in the round pen, where lameness will usually reveal itself in the horse's movement. In the meantime, my initial opinions are made fairly rapidly just as they will for the judge's first impression.

THE FACE

Standing directly in front of the horse, I begin with the horse's face as this is the first thing a judge sees as he watches the horse come in the pen. I want intelligent, large, soft eyes set wide on an attractive head. The ears should also contribute to an overall pleasant look. Both the ears and the eyes tell me a lot about the horse's disposition. Does the horse pin his ears as I or another horse approach? If so, he might have a bad attitude which interferes with his job as a pleasure horse no matter how well he moves. Are his eyes small and close-set? This often indicates lack of intelligence and poor visual capacity. Does the horse roll his eyes while constantly twitching his ears? I would suspect this horse is nervous and distrusting which does not make for a good pleasure horse candidate.

THE PROFILE

After looking at the horse while he's directly in front of me, I move around to see the horse's throat latch, neck, shoulder and topline in a profile position. In the show pen, this is a judge's next view as the horse comes through the entrance and turns to move down the rail. I like to see a horse's head come into the neck with a nice, clean throat latch. "Clean" describes a neck which is not thick or meaty looking. A long, clean neck should extend out from the withers. The best way to gauge this is to look at the horse's overall topline. Ideally a pleasure

This two-year-old has a pretty head, a clean throat latch and a long neck which ties into his withers nicely.

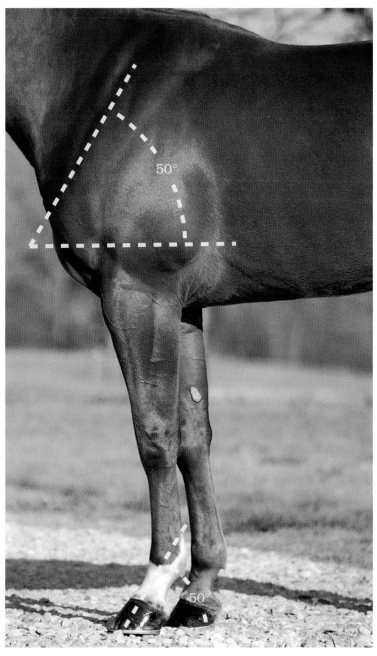

The angle of the shoulder and the angle of the pastern should match.

horse carries his head and neck so that a straight line is formed from the horse's ear to the withers to the top of the hip. A horse who moves around the pasture carrying his head and neck close to this position is much easier to train and ultimately makes a much better pleasure horse than the horse whose natural head carriage resembles a giraffe.

The horse's neck is critical to the horse's sense of balance. A pleasure horse should have a long, slim neck that is proportionately equal to the rest of the horse's body because the neck is used as a sort of balance arm to steady the body as the legs swing underneath.

With the shoulder, I'm primarily interested in its angle since the degree of slope to a horse's shoulder determines the length of the horse's stride. Ideally a horse's shoulder should have a 45 degree or slightly greater angle. Too little slope makes the horse short-strided. Too much slope results in a stride which is too long. Furthermore, since the angle of the shoulder and the angle of the pastern should match, a horse with a great deal of slope to its shoulder also tends to have a pastern which is too long. This creates a springy, sinking action in the horse's step which is undesirable. The angle of the shoulder should also match the angle of the hip, but I'll discuss that later in this chapter.

This horse has a nice profile and is well-balanced. His clean neck is proportionate to his body; his back is relatively short and he has a nice hip and low hocks.

To finish out the overall impression of the profile, I look for a strong, short back, a nice long hip and good, low-set hocks. Let's begin with the back. A few horses with long backs make good pleasure horses, but more often a long-backed horse struggles to keep his front end and his back end in sync with one another. These horses are also often weak in the back, i.e., it appears to sink downward between the withers and the top of the hip. Therefore the horse really labors to carry a rider's weight. This is evident when the horse's back "hollows out," meaning the horse raises his head and neck, looses the lifted arch in his back and allows it to drop. The back legs then tend to hang out behind the point of the hip, rather than reaching deeply under the horse's body, as the horse jogs or lopes.

The hips provide the horse with the power necessary to create impulsion in the hind legs. Impulsion is critical to a horse's ability to lope, and I explain this in detail when covering how to evaluate movement. At this point, just keep in mind that while a pleasure horse's hip is seldom going to be as muscular as a halter horse's, it should be sufficiently long and strong.

With the hocks, I like them to be set low to the ground and in a straight line down from the hip. Hocks with "too much set" are those in which the joint is formed so that it positions the lower part of the leg too far under the horse's body. Horses with this type of conformation are notoriously bad joggers.

These hocks have "too much set." The joint positions the lower part of the leg too far under the horse's body.

BALANCE

Finally, I look at how well the front half of the horse and the back half match. This is important for the sake of appearance, as well as for evaluating ability. A well-balanced horse usually has a short back, a long underline and matching shoulder and hip angles. Because a proportionately structured frame allows for the physical coordination necessary in any athletic event, balance is important for all performance horses and has come to be the basis on which conformation is judged.

EVALUATING MOVEMENT

After forming my first impressions on a prospect's appearance, I evaluate movement. I first like to see the prospect turned loose in an area where I can chase him around and watch him move on his own. I like to see yearlings out in the pasture. With the older prospects, I usually watch them while turned loose in a round pen or arena. In either case the object is to look at natural ability.

If I see the yearlings as a group in the pasture it also allows me to watch for attitude around other horses as well as movement. Remember to take into consideration how fresh these colts may be. I give them time to gallop back and forth a few times while they get used to new people in their pasture. Also, many people tend to favor the horse that hangs back from the rest of the group as they move across a field. In theory that might work, but

Watching a group of yearlings in the pasture gives the prospective buyer a chance to watch for attitude around other horses as well as movement.

in reality I think you have to remember that one may stay back from the herd because he's afraid of other horses or because he ran and played earlier that day and simply isn't as fresh as the others. Examine each colt as an individual within a group.

Since western pleasure is ideally a natural event, i.e., we're not asking the horses to do anything they can't or won't do on their own, I obviously look for the same qualities in a prospect as I do when judging older pleasure horses in the show pen. They should demonstrate an ability, as well as a desire, to walk, jog and lope softly and gracefully. If a prospect takes short, quick strides with his head up and his nose stuck straight out, you can be sure it won't be easy for him to lope slowly with his neck level when you're on his back. And even if you can train him to do so, he'll almost certainly never perform well enough to beat those who do so naturally.

THE PROSPECT'S JOG

As a horse jogs off in the pasture or turnout area, I first watch the hind legs. I want a prospect to keep his feet underneath his body at the jog. I make sure the hocks aren't left out behind the point of the hip, and I don't want to see a horse drag or scuff his hooves across the top of the dirt. Both of these characteristics indicate that the horse will be a weak jogger, particularly when the weight of a rider is added. I look at the front end to make sure the horse isn't shuffling along, but rather is holding his front end up and swinging the front legs from the shoulder with little knee action and a relatively short stride that closely matches his stride behind. Naturally, I'm also checking for lameness.

It's important to note that I don't necessarily rule out a prospect because I think it might be a weak jogger. I take note of that weakness, but I also watch it lope. In western pleasure, a horse's jog can often be improved through training and shoeing, but usually the lope must come naturally. This event is also judged more predominately on the lope. Sometimes this allows for mediocre joggers to win if they are great lopers.

THE PROSPECT'S LOPE

At the lope, I'm again going to watch the hind end first. I want to see the hind feet land flat and deep. I don't want to see a lot of movement in the hocks. Those back legs should simply be swinging slowly, smoothly and deeply under the horse's body. The horse should have a natural, easy flow to each stride as opposed to a quick, choppy stride. Softness is also critical at the lope. I almost want to be able to close my eyes and have the horse lope by without me even hearing him hit the ground.

This horse's legs are doing exactly what Doug wants out of his horse at the lope. He wants to see the hind feet land flat and deep. The front legs swing forward from the shoulder and reach full-extension before striking the ground.

Some people tend to criticize a western pleasure horse solely by his "knee." This is a term used to describe the amount of bend a horse has in its front legs, particularly at the lope. It's important to understand why I'm so critical of the hind end and fairly forgiving about the front legs. I've never had a judge come up to me and tell me he liked my horse except that he has too much knee. Usually, if a horse is good with his hind legs, he eventually flattens out up front. In other words, he uses his front leg without bending it very much at the knee. More importantly, the hind end controls speed as well as the steadiness of the head and neck. If the horse is really driving from behind, he's rolling everything forward, drops his head and neck on his own, and has plenty of time to extend that front leg to full extension before the foot strikes the ground. I therefore believe that if a horse is good with its hind end, the front end usually takes care of itself. Of course there are exceptions to every rule, but generally speaking this theory has worked for me.

ATTITUDE

Throughout this process, I watch the horses' attitudes and personalities, particularly when I'm watching a group of yearlings. I want to see a horse react well to other horses rather than pinning his ears or charging maliciously. After I move the herd around a few times, I go out among them and perhaps touch them to see how they react to me. It's okay if a horse is initially a little scared of me, but within a few minutes of moving around him and touching him, he should react well to me. I like that. I don't expect them all to just stand there calmly and quietly. In fact, I really don't want a complete "dead head." I find that since those types don't care about anything, they usually don't care about being ridden. They have little or no expression in the arena. I look for the horse with an interested, intelligent expression.

SOUNDNESS

After I select the prospects which fit my criteria, I closely examine legs for soundness and then see how a horse carries himself in a controlled environment. Soundness is mandatory. Yet, a western pleasure horse doesn't perform at the level of physical intensity as a race horse or a reiner, for example, so absolute correctness in a pleasure horse's legs is perhaps not as critical as it is for those horses. Plenty of pleasure horses with less than perfect conformation have loped out of the line-up first. Yet some standards are necessary in order for pleasure horses to perform gracefully.

Inspecting the legs, I want to see that they are relatively "clean" in the sense that they aren't disfigured with bumps or swelling around the joints which indicate weaknesses. With the average horse, this type of visual inspection for weaknesses is sufficient. If anything looks questionable, i.e., I see unusual bumps, scars or swollen joints, I require a veterinarian's examination and radiographs.

Strong, healthy hooves are as important to a horse as the tires on a car. Everything ultimately rides on them. The hooves should be a sufficient size in relation to the horse's body. Unfortunately, small feet became a popular trend within the Quarter Horse industry many years ago. Today, some pleasure and halter horses in particular, now pay the price for that fad in the form of widespread lameness. I've seldom seen a horse whose feet were too big.

EVALUATING THE YEARLING INDIVIDUALLY

After watching the yearlings move around their pasture as a group, I like to separate them from the herd and take them into a round pen individually. As in the pasture, I again study the legs at a jog and lope with the yearling turned loose in the round pen. Here I either confirm that a horse is a good mover or determine that he's not, using the same standards and theories that applied while watching the yearling in the pasture. As always, I am particularly interested in natural head carriage, hoping to see the horse carry his head out long and low in front of himself for reasons described earlier.

OBSERVING THE PROSPECT UNDER SADDLE

With a green broke two-year-old I have the advantage of seeing how the horse moves with weight on his back. This can make quite a difference. Many people gamble by purchasing colts in the fall because they're less expensive, but that's where the old saying, "Cheap is expensive," often applies. Personally, I prefer to wait and buy a horse when I can watch somebody ride it, even if I have to pay a little more. I'd simply rather give more for a horse and know what I'm buying.

I begin my evaluation before the horse is saddled by quickly studying his physical characteristics as described earlier, and then checking for soundness as I watch the horse move freely in a round pen. If I like what I've seen thus far, I watch someone ride the horse in the round pen. Again, this provides a controlled environment in which to study the legs. I look for the same qualities in a green-broke two-year-old as I did in a yearling prospect: a jog without any dragging feet or hocks left behind the body; a soft, sweeping lope that begins with hind legs which land flatly and deeply under the horse's body; and good, natural head carriage.

I also want to see the horse ridden outside the round pen in a larger arena or an open field. I watch the horse perform on his own, without draw reins or a martingale or any type of training device other than a standard sidepull, snaffle bit or bridle. I know the horse won't pack his head and neck like an older, broker horse, but I want to see what he does when he's out on his own. Horses know the difference. I expect his head to come up slightly and his nose to go out, but I want to make sure it doesn't get out of control.

I not only watch movement, I also study attitude. Does the horse swish his tail excessively or pin his ears?

I continue to monitor this when I ride the horse. I pick up on the reins and use my legs to move the horse around. Is the horse uncomfortable with this or does he willingly accept my guidance? How does the horse react to new sights outside the arena? I expect a horse to look at a piece of paper blowing across the ground for example, but I don't want him to stop and stare and loose all concentration on what I'm asking him to do.

Regarding speed, I don't expect all colts to start off jogging or loping slowly. Some will, but many won't. If a horse starts off fast however, I do expect him to slow himself down after four or five strides. This tells me the horse has a natural rate and will eventually choose to go slow on his own.

WHAT TO LOOK FOR IN AN OLDER PLEASURE HORSE

This chapter has primarily been geared toward selecting a pleasure horse prospect, however the theories and advice I expressed here are also applicable toward buying an older pleasure horse. Soundness and breeding are again important. I also like to use the same procedure of establishing a first impression, and I still want to see the horse move while turned loose in an arena or pasture so I can evaluate natural ability.

When the horse is saddled, I again watch someone else ride the horse and then ride it myself. At this point, I'm judging the horse on movement, disposition and brokeness. All of these qualities are relative to the horse's age, my goals for a particular horse and the cost of that horse. For example, if I'm looking at a very expensive three-year-old mare for one of my amateurs to show at major futurities, my standards are quite different than if I'm looking at a twelve-year-old gelding for a youth to show in novice classes. Generally speaking however, I want to see that the horse is qualified for the job I'm going to employ him to do, at the price I'm willing and able to pay. This is purely up to the individual.

FINDING A PLEASURE PROSPECT IN THE LONGE LINE CLASS

In 1990, Tom Powers, who puts on one of the oldest and most prestigious pleasure futurities in the country, invented the Longe Line class. The class was designed to give people a place to compete with and market their pleasure prospects as yearlings. Each entry is allowed 90 seconds to demonstrate the walk, jog and lope in both directions, and then the entries are lined up in halter class fashion and judged on conformation in regard to balance and athletic ability. The Yearling Longe Line class is now a very popular NSBA approved event offered at most all pleasure futurities as well as at many breed association shows.

For someone looking to buy a pleasure prospect, this class is great for several reasons. First, yearlings by many different stallions are gathered in one place where people can compare them, rather than the prospective buyer having to travel all over the country to separate locations. Also, the buyer sees the colts when they are cleaned up and presented at their best, rather than out in the rough somewhere. Since the horses are each presented on the same day in the same show ring, the environment also becomes less of a factor than it may be when the prospective buyer is going to many different farms. For example, he won't see one colt in the snow and bitter cold in Iowa and have to compare it to a colt in a green pasture in sunny Florida.

It should be noted that just because a yearling does well in this class does not guarantee it will do well under saddle. Until you've seen a horse with weight on his back, it's always a gamble. And colts grow and change a great deal as they mature from a yearling to a two-year-old. But if a person wants to buy a yearling and take a chance, I highly suggest watching the Longe Line class for a colt which meets the criteria I've described in this chapter.

GENERAL THEORY ON BUYING HORSES

Finally, I have a general theory on buying horses. It applies to horses of any age, but seems particularly useful when selecting young pleasure prospects. After closely examining a prospect in relation to all of the points I discussed in this chapter, I usually leave that horse and wait to make any decisions until after I've come back and looked a second time. Sometimes I may leave a ranch and come back later that day, and sometimes I wait until the next day or even a week later. I believe a person is more critical of a prospect the second time he sees it, so if he buys the horse after just one look, that re-evaluation may come too late. When I like a horse more the second time than I did the first, that prospect usually works out well.

4

Pleasure Horse Pre-School: Establishing Trust

Much like a child's education begins in pre-school and kindergarten, a pleasure horse's training is founded while the colt is still a weanling and a yearling. These early sessions are as important to the horse's career as later lessons which include a saddle. We're teaching manners and familiarizing him with basic concepts like standing while ground tied and longing. Most importantly, we're establishing trust. It is during these days that a horse's attitude is formed toward the humans who will handle him for the rest of his life.

I think it's best for a colt to spend most of his days out in the pasture with a group of colts after weaning and throughout most of the yearling year because the colts play together and learn to relate to one another. If a person only has one colt, I even suggest buying an inexpensive goat just to put out in the pasture with the youngster to give him some company and teach him to interact with another animal. A young horse with this kind of foundation develops a better attitude toward other horses because he's used to being in a group. On the other hand, a colt who grows up in a stall by himself is like a sheltered child. It's important for a pleasure horse to be comfortable around other horses since he won't be performing alone as a show horse. Besides, a child needs time to just be a kid, and the same holds true for a colt.

I occasionally bring the weanlings and early yearlings into the barn for individual handling. When this actually begins and how often it occurs simply depends on a person's individual schedule. Usually the earlier in a colt's life that he's handled the better because he's less set in his ways and also smaller so therefore easier to handle. I

recommend working with a colt as often as a person's schedule allows; perhaps weekly, once a month or every sixty days, which is when they need to be wormed and have their feet trimmed. Sometimes I keep a colt up in the barn for a few days or maybe even a week so I can work with him. This is especially important for the yearlings. The more I handle them in the spring and summer, the easier it is for me and the colts when I begin riding them in the fall. A scared or rebellious colt is less likely to injure me or himself now than when he is a bigger, stronger horse.

These periods when the colt is kept up and handled also give me a chance to learn individual likes and dislikes. If I see a colt is touchy about his ears, for example, I tackle that problem early by spending a lot of time softly brushing and rubbing around his face and ears. This may eliminate problems when as an older horse, he has to tolerate his ears being clipped and cleaned out as part of the normal grooming procedure for a show horse. Some colts become nervous or scared when their feet are picked up and held as the farrier does to trim them. If, as part of the normal grooming procedure, I patiently pick up each of his feet and hold them for just a minute or so while rubbing his shoulder or back, he soon learns that this is not a bad experience. This lesson comes in handy every time the farrier works on the horse's feet for the rest of his life.

By using this time working with a colt to evaluate his attitude, I am able to correct problems by tackling them early on and being persistent about fixing them. If a colt who is tied in his stall or the round pen shows me that he resents me, by pinning his ears or pulling back on the rope, I walk right up to him and start petting and rubbing on him. He may hate being touched and fight to escape it. But I continue touching him, petting and rubbing him all over, until he relaxes and realizes that being touched isn't so bad. If a colt bites or kicks at me, I reprimand him by immediately swatting him on the shoulder or hindquarters with a longing whip. I give him one smack and then allow the colt just a second or two to think about it. Then I go right back to doing whatever I was doing when the colt bit or kicked. If he tries it again, I hit him with the whip again. Before long the colt associates kicking with the sting of the whip and figures out that it hurts him to bite or kick me.

Early sessions are made up of a lot of hand walking, brushing, picking up the feet and an introduction to longing. Everything is done patiently and quietly. I want a colt to respect me, so I don't spoil or coddle him. I also want him to trust me. Therefore, I go about everything calmly and efficiently.

LEARNING TO GROUND TIE

This is a good time to teach a colt to "ground tie," meaning he stands still in the hallway of the barn without being tied to anything. This concept comes in handy

(pages 42-43) A colt needs time to just be a colt.

(opposite) Because these colts will grow up together rather than being isolated in stalls, they will likely develop a good attitude toward other horses.

when the horse is older and many circumstances require him to stand still. Since ground tieing is often used while brushing and saddling horses, I use the grooming sessions with the colt now to also teach him to ground tie. The colt is more likely to relax and stand still if he's thinking about how good the brush feels.

Start by positioning him in the center of the aisle where he isn't tempted by nearby brushes or tack. Drop the lead rope in front of him and firmly tell him "whoa." Begin brushing his face and neck while the colts stands quietly. As you move toward his shoulder and back, occasionally repeat the word "whoa" and expect him to stand without moving his feet. If he does move, quietly reach for the lead rope and push him back to his position. Tell him "whoa" again and then go back to work. At first, don't ask him to stand there for long periods, perhaps only three or four minutes, but after only a few lessons the colt understands that he must stand quietly while you brush him.

Since these lessons come at different times for different colts depending on your schedule or even when you purchased a colt, use patience and good judgement to guide you. A weanling should not be expected to stand there like an older horse. But with the older colts who've been in this program for a few months, I expect a little more.

If they absolutely won't stand still and obviously are not paying attention, I may get after them a little bit by putting a chain over the nose and tugging on that as I push them back into place and tell them "whoa." I demand their respect, but I don't expect a horse to be perfect if he hasn't been given a chance to learn how to behave properly. I use a chain only in severe cases, and then I am extremely cautious not to provoke the horse into getting panic stricken and perhaps hurting me or himself.

SACKING OUT THE COLT

Once the colt understands the concept of standing ground tied while being groomed and is used to the surroundings in the barn, I start "sacking out" the colt each time I handle him. This involves taking an empty feed sack, a rain slicker or even a saddle blanket and rubbing it all over the horse's body and head while requiring the horse to stand still. It teaches the horse to resist the urge to run away from something he's frightened of and to trust the handler.

Begin by slowly and gently rubbing the sack against the horse's shoulder and gradually moving it over the horse's back and hip. Then bring it forward over the neck and eventually even the head. Keep repeating the word "whoa" in a firm yet reassuring tone. If he moves from the ground tied position, put him back in place immediately. As this is done over and over, the colt learns that nothing is going to hurt him. You earn the colt's trust and also desensitize him to his surroundings.

The colt is "sacked out" for the first time in the round pen. Using a saddle blanket, Doug rubs the horse's body while requiring the horse to stand still. It teaches the horse to resist the urge to run away from something he's frightened of and to trust the handler.

LONGING

I don't longe weanlings simply because it's too stressful on their young bones and joints and may create lameness. In the early part of a colt's yearling year, longing is used only for exercise and as a means of teaching them a few basic commands. It gives me an opportunity to evaluate both their abilities at the jog and the lope, but only from the same perspectives I use in selecting a prospect. In other words, I'm looking for naturally level head carriage as well as soft, even strides rather than short, choppy ones. I'm not worried about speed, and I don't use any kind of training device to set their heads when they're this young.

Longing also teaches a colt to respond to my commands for the walk, jog, lope and halt. He's ready for this lesson at most any stage in his yearling year. As in each of the lessons he's learning at this age including being groomed, leading quietly, standing patiently, etc., quiet but firm handling teaches a colt that it's time to work and you're the boss.

By teaching the longing routine, you incorporate exercise with training early in the horse's education.

It's easiest to teach a colt to longe while he's turned loose in a round pen, but if you don't have one then use the following instructions while working the colt on a longe line in the middle of your riding arena. For a young colt, I normally don't put a chain over or under the nose unless I need the added control.

The ideal round pen is 50 or 60 feet in diameter. My pen has solid, six foot high walls so the horse doesn't have any distractions from outside. A round pen is preferable over a rectangular arena because it doesn't have corners for a horse to think about turning. It also doesn't offer him anywhere to stop and attempt to hide by facing into the corner.

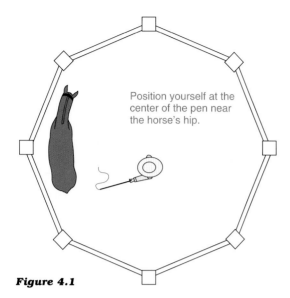

Position yourself at the center of the pen near the horse's hip.

Figure 4.1

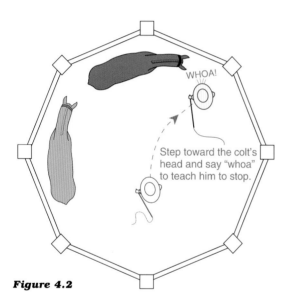

WHOA!

Step toward the colt's head and say "whoa" to teach him to stop.

Figure 4.2

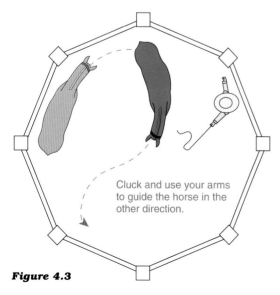

Cluck and use your arms to guide the horse in the other direction.

Figure 4.3

Begin by leading the colt to the round pen wall so his body is parallel with the wall and ready to move forward along the wall. Unsnap the lead line, and quietly step back toward the center of the pen, positioning yourself near the horse's hip (see figure 4.1). Make sure you're not so close that you might be kicked. Remain in this position throughout the longing process. (If you're not in a round pen, get a mental image of the circular path on which you want the colt to move around you. Position the colt on that path, facing in the direction you want him to go and then step back to the position described above.)

The colt may run and buck upon discovering that he's turned loose. This is fine. Allowing the colt time to get rid of this excess energy is only fair to a youngster, and it improves his ability to pay attention to the handler for the remainder of the session. When he's through playing, simply resume your position at his hip with the horse facing the direction you want him to go and proceed.

The horse is encouraged to walk forward by the subtle use of a lead rope or longing whip. Don't do anything which might startle the colt, but by gently tapping his hip with the rope or the whip you get his attention and urge him to move forward. If he's still a little fresh he may take off running, but he'll soon be out of energy and will be content to walk. The lazier colts always prefer just to walk or stand still. The more lively ones have to learn to start off at a walk rather than a run, but they usually catch on to that idea after just a few sessions.

Teach the colt to trot by making a clucking noise and again using the rope or whip to urge the colt forward. To ask for a lope, make a "kissing" noise and encourage the horse to move faster by gently swinging or touching his hip with the lead rope or whip. Try to remain in the original position at the horse's hip — you may need to "chase" the colt a little by increasing the length and speed of your steps as you and the colt move around the circle. After just a few lessons you can basically stay more toward the center of the circle as the colt learns to jog and lope solely off sound cues.

I begin teaching the colt to halt after he moves around the pen a few times and appears ready to quit. Say "whoa" as you step toward his head and neck, almost in front of him, so he's thinking about your position and stops (see figure 4.2). After repeating this a few times, he soon associates "whoa" with stopping and wondering what you're going to do next.

To turn the colt in the other direction, first ask the colt to stop. He should be looking toward you or may even be facing you if you've instilled in him a tendency to wonder what your next move will be. Move further in front of the colt to discourage him from moving forward. Clucking and using your arms to guide him back in the other direction, urge him to turn and move in the opposite direction (see figure 4.3). If you're working him on the line, use it to pull the horse around.

It isn't difficult for a colt to learn how to longe in this manner. By the second or third lesson, he'll respond to the cues like most older horses. Ideally, the yearling is turned out in a pasture as I described earlier, so these longing sessions are not his only means of exercise. Therefore he only needs about five or ten minutes of longing each time he is brought up to the barn for handling. If the yearling is kept in a stall, I suggest turning him out to play for several hours each day in a paddock or round pen, and then longing him for five to ten minutes every other day or so. By teaching a yearling the longing routine, you incorporate exercise with training early in the horse's education. It is also a means of exercise that a horse will be exposed to throughout his life as a pleasure horse.

THE REWARDS OF EARLY EDUCATION

While the reasons for handling a colt in the manner I've described may seem obvious, consider their importance. A weanling or a yearling who isn't handled patiently and quietly is often nervous or belligerent when he officially goes into training in the fall prior to his two-year-old year. Rather than breaking him to ride, the trainer first must spend early sessions trying to overcome these problems. The horse may never have a great attitude. Furthermore, a yearling who has never been handled usually suffers from what I call "the thirty day recession" when I start riding him. By that I mean he is in such a state of shock about so many new sights and ideas that he suffers physically as well as mentally. In other words, a horse won't move like he should if he's too stressed about his environment. A horse who is comfortable with me and his surroundings quickly adjusts to being ridden. He shows me his true potential as a mover.

Consider time spent with a weanling or a yearling as both time and money saved when that horse is a two-year-old. By simply bringing a colt up from the pasture and working with him even once a month throughout his yearling year, you probably save at least thirty days in the breaking process. If you're paying a trainer, that's significant money. Time spent with a colt before he's ridden simply gives that colt an early career advantage.

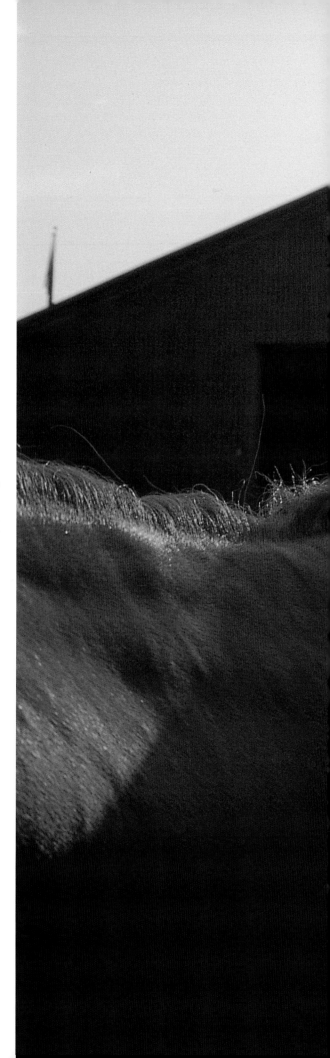

"PROPER HEAD CARRIAGE SHOULD BE ESTABLISHED BEFORE THE COLT IS RIDDEN."

5

The Two-Year-Old: Preparation for Breaking

Preparation for a pleasure horse's two-year-old year begins in the fall while he's still a yearling. The futurities and AQHA classes start July 1, and it's best to allow a full six months for breaking and training. Ultimately however, the schedule for breaking a colt depends on the colt himself.

The first steps in preparing a horse for breaking are: making sure his teeth and feet are in good shape; evaluating physical maturity; introducing the horse to the bit; and assessing conformation in regard to head carriage.

DENTAL WORK

If a horse's teeth are in bad shape, he can't eat and he won't want to work. A two-year-old's mouth should be checked for sharp points which need to be filed down, which is called being "floated." Most horses also have wolf teeth which need to be pulled at this age. Wolf teeth are small teeth that develop in front of the horse's molars. They have no purpose and are painful if bumped by the bit. Since all communication from the rider's hands goes through the horse's mouth, it's important that the mouth doesn't hurt.

FARRIER WORK

Shoeing a two-year-old depends on the individual horse's feet. If they're prone to chipping and cracking or if they become tender from increased wear when he goes into training, I use regular light weight steel shoes. This is normally only necessary on the front feet which carry most of the horse's weight. You can find more information about shoeing your horse in Chapter 15, "Tips on Shoeing," which covers this topic in greater detail.

(above and opposite top) Both of these horses are two-year-olds, however the bay's gangly, coltish appearance (above) indicates that he is too weak and physically immature to start breaking. The sorrel (opposite) has a stronger, more mature structure and is ready to start.

(pages 50-51) Doug teaches a horse who doesn't naturally carry his head level to give to the bridle with the aid of a bitting rig before he's ridden.

DETERMINING IF THE HORSE IS READY TO RIDE

I evaluate yearlings in the early fall to determine if they're ready for the breaking process. If the horse appears to be physically weak and immature, I leave him out in the pasture until December or January or whenever he's ready to be put into a training program. A colt with a fine bone structure and an overall gangly, coltish appearance is not strong enough to be ridden. Some colts also go through growing stages in which their hips are much higher than their withers. This makes it difficult for them to use themselves properly, so I try to wait until the front end catches up with the back end again. I want a colt to have strong, well-developed legs and the more balanced, mature look of an older horse.

Many times my evaluation of a horse's maturity is influenced after I ride him for the first few times. He may seem strong when I'm standing on the ground looking at him, but if he really struggles to carry my weight, he's telling me I need to wait at least another month or so before beginning any serious riding.

Some horses simply don't make that July 1 deadline, and that's okay. I can wait and bring a horse out at the later fall futurities, or I may wait until he is a three-year-old to begin showing him. The horse is my first priority. If he's pushed and shown too early, he suffers mentally and physically. He won't perform well as a two-year-old or later in his career.

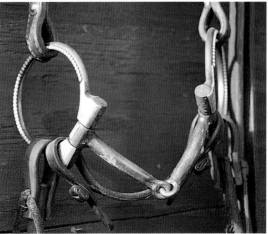

(above) Doug prefers to break his colts using a smooth snaffle bit.

(left) The bit should "hang" slightly in the mouth so that it fits gently in the corner of the mouth without forming any wrinkles.

INTRODUCING THE BIT

If the horse appears ready to progess in my program, the next step is to introduce the bit. Depending on whether I'm ready to ride the horse or plan to work him in a bitting rig first, which I explain later in this chapter, the introduction to the bit may take place on the same day as my first ride or weeks before. I should also mention that I personally prefer a smooth snaffle bit rather than a sidepull for breaking my colts because a snaffle offers more control. The snaffle bit is mild enough for a young horse's mouth and is also appropriate for use with the bitting rig.

To get the horse accustomed to the bit, I slip a head-stall with a plain 5/8-inch, O-ring or D-ring, smooth snaffle bit, on his head. The bit should "hang" slightly in the mouth so that it fits gently in the corner of the mouth without forming any wrinkles. I usually remove the reins from the bit, and then either turn him loose in the round pen or attach the longe line to the inside ring of the bit. The horse is then longed as normal. He may chew and mouth the bit at first, but after just a few longing sessions while wearing the bit he learns to accept it or eventually forgets about it when given other things to think about in the breaking process.

EVALUATING NATURAL HEAD CARRIAGE

My program for breaking colts is different from those of many other pleasure horse trainers in that I believe proper head carriage should be established before the colt is ever ridden. In the show pen, a pleasure horse is expected to carry his head so that his poll is level with his withers. His face should be fairly close to vertical with the ground, and there will be slack in the reins. I refer to this as "packing the bit." These characteristics aid movement by helping a horse balance himself. They also cause him to round his back, thereby causing him to drive his hocks more deeply under his body.

Determining whether a horse naturally carries his head in this position is relatively easy. Study the horse's conformation and how he carries his head and neck while he is relaxed. If he's fresh or excited as on a cold winter morning or after being kept up in a stall for a few days, you won't make an accurate assessment. Over a period of several days or even weeks, I look at the horse while he's standing still either in his stall or the pasture, while he's being longed in the round pen, and while he's leisurely moving out in the pasture.

Ideally, I want to see the horse's neck come out of his withers flat so that a profile view gives the appearance of a straight, flat line from the base of the ears all the way back to the top of the hip. The flatter the topline as the horse moves, the better. Furthermore, the front of the horse's face should be fairly close to vertical. This horse will naturally adapt to packing the bit when he's ridden.

On the other hand, the horse who is not likely to naturally carry his head properly has the following characteristics: his profile is almost "L" shaped, so that the neck is closer to being perpendicular with the back than it is to being a continuation of the back's flat line; and the face is closer to being parallel with the ground than it is begin perpendicular with it. This doesn't necessarily mean this horse can't move well with his head and neck in the proper position, but he needs help learning how.

I should also explain that horses who naturally carry their heads in the same position as it should be in the show pen are usually easier to train. Yet plenty of good horses started off as colts who carried their heads a little high. It's comparable to a basketball player who is much shorter than his teammates. He isn't ideally suited for the sport, but with determination and dedicated practice he develops the skills necessary to overcome his physical disadvantage. With any athlete, human or equine, this is often where attitude and "heart" become factors.

The remainder of this chapter is instruction on my concept of establishing proper head carriage before the horse is ridden. This may take one week or it might take sixty days. I define the steps taken in this program based on the average horse. Some horses are exceptionally willing and take less time. Others are more rebellious and require more time. In any case, I wait for the horse to show me he's ready to move on. The next step in breaking a young horse is explained in Chapter 6 "Under Saddle." If your horse has a good, natural head carriage, skip the following section and advance to Chapter 6.

ESTABLISHING HEAD CARRIAGE FIRST

I teach a horse who doesn't naturally carry his head level to give to the bridle with the aid of a bitting rig before he's ridden. This prevents a battle once I'm on his back. A horse needs the first thirty days under saddle to become comfortable with carrying a person's weight. The horse can't do this if I'm constantly pulling on the reins trying to bring his head down and his nose in. If I allow him to keep his head up and his nose stuck out for the first couple of weeks, he becomes comfortable moving like this and thinks it is the way he's supposed to go. When I ask him to drop his head and pack the bit, he'll be confused and uncomfortable. The horse has enough to worry about when you're on his back, why not conquer the inevitable before then?

My objectives with this part of the program are to get the horse comfortable moving with his head in the correct position and to teach him to drop his head into the bit when I take a hold of him once I'm on his back.

A bitting rig, called a surcingle, is used to teach the horse where to carry his head. It is basically just a wide leather girth which reaches all the way around a horse's belly and back. It is placed on top of a regular saddle pad and sits just behind the withers so that the portion under the belly is in the same position as a saddle's girth. It should fit snugly to prevent it from slipping but not be so tight as to cause discomfort for the horse.

Some people use a regular work saddle for bitting a horse up, attaching the reins to the rings normally used to attach a breast collar to the saddle. I prefer a surcingle because its many rings allow me to vary the positions of the horse's head and neck. Determining which rings to use depends on the individual horse's conformation, and it changes as the horse progresses in this program. Generally, I try to tie the horse so that his head and neck

(above) Because this horse does not naturally carry his head level, Doug uses a surcingle to teach the horse where to carry his head.

(right) As the lessons in the bitting rig advance and the reins are tightened to teach the horse to pack the bit, his neck will tend to bow a little more than is ideal.

are put into the same position I want them to be in once I'm on his back. As the lessons in a bitting rig advance and the reins are tightened to teach the horse to pack the bit, his neck will tend to bow a little more than is ideal. Once I'm on his back, however, the neck levels back out. At this point, I'm just using the bitting rig to teach the horse that he can move properly and comfortably with his head and neck in front of his body rather than above it.

Before setting the horse up in the bitting rig for the first time, I let him get comfortable with having a bit in his mouth while he's being longed, as explained earlier in this chapter. Each session begins by allowing the horse enough "free time" in the round pen to work off any excess energy. He may have the bit in his mouth with the reins tied loosely to the surcingle so that he can use his head and neck freely without bumping his mouth against the bit. Or, if I think the horse will really run and buck, I may let him get rid of some of that energy before I even put the bit in his mouth. I don't want to take a chance on him injuring himself if he's playing hard.

For the first few sessions in the bitting rig, I prefer to turn the horse loose in the round pen because the horse may be a little nervous, and working without a line in the round pen is a little easier. However if you don't have a round pen, you must start off using a longe line attached to the bit's ring on the inside of the longing circle. If you start off with a longe line attached to the bit however, be careful not to pull so hard or quick as to startle the horse. For the first sessions in particular, try to use your contact with the horse's mouth only to gently guide the horse in a circle. Rely on your voice commands to ask the horse to stop, rather than pulling on his mouth.

The snaffle bit reins attach to the rings on the surcingle, either using specially made reins with elastic and snaps or by tieing regular reins to the rings. I try to position his head and neck as close to level as possible. Throughout the process, I study how the horse carries his head while in the bitting rig, and I adjust where the reins attach to the surcingle to keep the horse in the correct position. Initially, the reins are tied so that there is no real slack in them, but without much tension pulling his head down and his face in. I allow him to get comfortable with the bitting rig first.

I begin by asking the colt to walk, jog and halt. I use a longe whip and stand near the horse's hip as I did while longing the yearlings for exercise. By clucking and tapping his hip with the whip, I ask the colt to walk forward. With that first step or two, he may be startled or confused when he raises his head or pushes his nose out and finds the bit's resistance. He may get mad and fight it or he may become sullen and refuse to go forward. This is natural. I remain patient but firm and eventually the horse figures out he can go forward.

Each of these sessions in the bitting rig will be as brief as possible. My goal each day is to work the horse both directions and to see some progress in his willingness to drop his head into the bit. This kind of work is physically and mentally strenuous for a horse, so I don't want to work him too hard or too long. As soon as I see progress, like some slack in the reins or an obvious willingness to drop his head and just go forward, I let him quit for the day on that positive note. Some days this may take only 10 minutes and on other days it may require 30 minutes of work, but I'm always looking for a good place to end the session.

Every day, I gradually tighten the reins, shortening the distance between the bit and the surcingle by about an inch each time. Eventually the length of the reins keeps the horse from poking his nose past vertical. The horse gives to the bit's pressure by flexing at the poll. Again, the reins attach to the surcingle at the points which hold the horse's neck close to level, however it's important to realize that his neck won't be completely level while he's learning to pack the bit. Through the rest of the breaking process, he learns to level out his neck further. If at any point the horse becomes extremely agitated and upset, I release some of the tension in the reins and work him at an easier level for a few days. When he's working comfortably, I gradually begin tightening the reins again.

For the horse being longed loose in the round pen, I work the horse for four or five days until he is responding well i.e., he is not resisting in any way. Then I attach a longe line to the bit's ring at the corner of the horse's mouth. With the longe line, I have a little more control and can pull on him real easy when I say "whoa" so that he stops and stands. This gets him even more accustomed to responding to pressure from the bit. If you started the horse on the longe line because you didn't have a round pen, begin gently pulling on the horse when you ask him to stop as soon as you feel the horse is responding well and ready for this new aspect to his training.

The next four to five days are spent walking, jogging, stopping and standing on the longe line. While the horse is standing still, I reverse him by attaching the longe line to the opposite side of his head, gently pulling him around to the inside and then asking him to walk forward now that he's facing the other direction.

The reins are tied short enough to keep his head in position, and he's getting comfortable with this new position. Gradually, I increase the mental aspect of his training by putting the horse in different situations which force him to think and react. For cxample, my cues to jog won't be as loud or as obvious, and I'll expect him to respond to my cues more quickly. I also may do some things that might startle the horse, like waving my arms wildly or shaking a feed sack. The horse's first reaction is usually to throw his head up in the air and take off running. But while in the bitting rig he soon figures out that he cannot throw his head up. It's also kind of like the sacking out

While being longed in the bitting rig, the horse learns to give to the bit's pressure by flexing at the poll.

procedure we used on the colt earlier where we eventually de-sensitize the horse to things that might ordinarily frighten him. The horse learns that there's nothing to be afraid of and that he can't escape, and so he just continues doing his job despite his surroundings. This is extremely valuable once he's a show horse on the rail.

After a week or sometimes two, the average horse is comfortable walking and jogging in the bitting rig on the longe line. He is not nervous or resistant. He is ready to lope. I begin by asking him to lope out of a jog by making the standard "kissing" noise and either cracking the whip or tapping his hip with it. At first he'll probably only lope about halfway around the arena and then break down into a trot. I let him come back down to a slow jog, ask him to halt and then let him stand there. The horse is usually a little nervous with this new gear. He isn't going to go around "picture perfect." He is a little quick underneath, and he looks a little uncoordinated. Allowing him to do things slowly and gradually with time to stand and relax in between will reassure him. It may take a week of doing this before he calmly and quietly lopes a full lap around the round pen.

Now I simply work the colt every day for fifteen minutes to a half an hour. Each day he should become more at ease and appear more coordinated at jogging and loping around the round pen while in the bitting rig. I expect him to respond to my cues promptly yet quietly. When he can lope around the arena comfortably until I ask him to stop, and he shows no signs of resistance such as furiously chewing the bit while pulling against the reins, or sitting back and refusing to go forward, he's ready to be ridden.

6

Under Saddle

If you have selected a suitable prospect for western pleasure and handled him so he respects and trusts you, this portion of the training program won't be difficult. It's merely a period in which the horse gets used to things like carrying weight and responding to cues which now come from someone on his back. None of this presents a problem for the typical pleasure prospect. Therefore you may soon find out if your horse isn't physically or mentally capable of being a pleasure horse. It may show up as a total lack of coordination or his refusal to slow down from a dead gallop to a lope.

The breaking process described in this chapter and the following one is often referred to as the "first thirty days," however it may take anywhere from two to eight weeks to accomplish my goals for this time period. Although the colt will be far from finished by the end of this phase in his training, this time is useful in evaluating what kind of horse I'll end up with. I may determine that he doesn't have the physical or mental ability to make a competitive pleasure horse. He has to have natural ability, so I don't waste my time if he doesn't. I sell him and go on to the next one. I may decide the colt is not mature enough to put into a rigorous training program and put him back out in the pasture for three to six more months. I'll make another evaluation then.

If I believe the colt has what it takes to make a nice horse, I proceed with the program explained in these chapters. First, however, I want to note that this is where the importance of how the horse was handled as a weanling and a yearling is often seen. When a colt is ground tied, groomed, sacked out, longed and just generally handled on a fairly frequent basis, he's far more mature

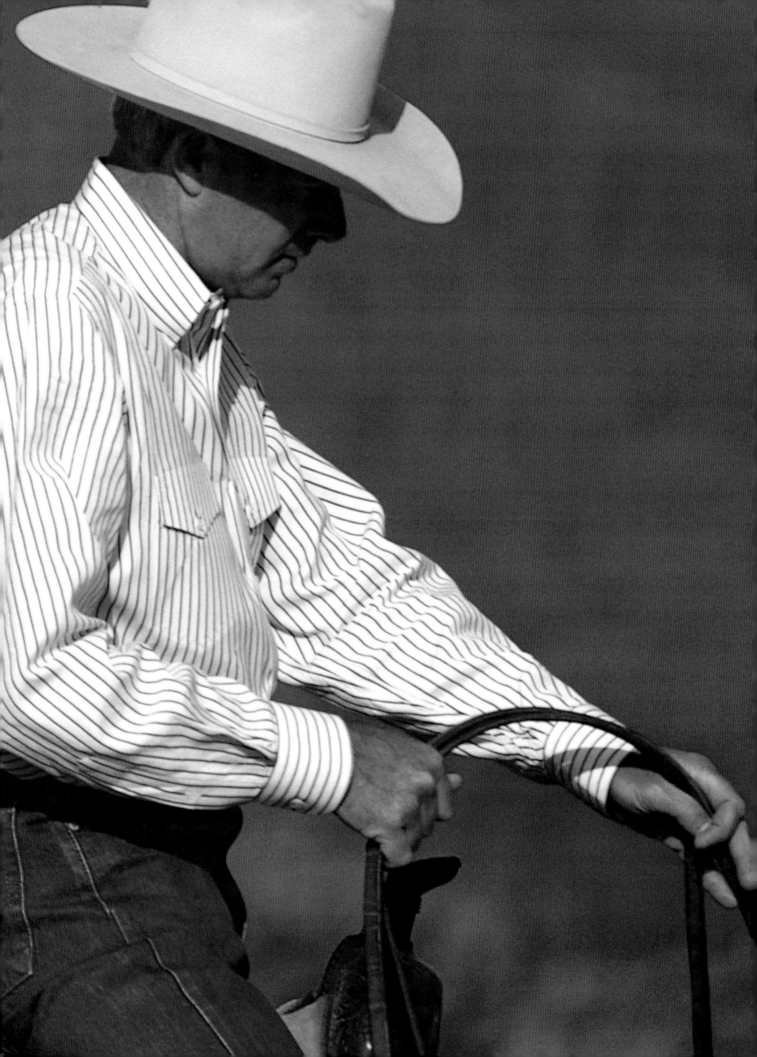

(pages 60-61) Using the outside rein and then following through with the inside rein, Doug teaches the concept of neck reining from the very first ride.

mentally than the colt who has been handled very little. A mentally mature colt accepts the saddle and the rider more readily and generally progresses faster in the early stages of a riding program.

THE FIRST SADDLING

The first saddling takes place in the stall or the round pen with the colt tied securely to a solid wall. The wall should be high enough that the colt can't get into trouble if he jumps forward, and he should be tied up close to the wall so he can't move around much. I've already longed him that day to get rid of any excess energy, so the colt stands quietly as I brush and move around him.

I don't believe in handling a horse timidly. Place the pad and the saddle on his back confidently. Many pleasure horses have such relaxed, laid-back attitudes that they really aren't bothered by the saddle. Some, however, are what we call "cold-backed," meaning they are inclined to buck when first saddled. You should be prepared if the horse does react nervously or rebelliously, but don't instigate it by treating him tentatively or roughly.

Doug places the saddle on the colt's back quietly but confidently.

Cinch up the saddle snugly but not too tightly at first. If the horse seems tense, I leave him tied in the stall with the saddle on his back for an hour or so. By then he'll probably accept it and I can proceed. If not, I may unsaddle him and follow the same procedure again the next day. When the colt is comfortable standing with the saddle on his back, he's ready to be longed while saddled.

If the colt was very quiet throughout the saddling procedure and readily accepted the saddle, it's okay to lead him while saddled. For a cold-backed colt however, I remove the saddle to lead him to the round pen and then re-saddle him once inside the pen. Otherwise he may tend to bolt coming out of the stall or while being lead to

With the colt still tied securely to the round pen wall, Doug puts his foot in the stirrup (a), pulls himself up halfway and then pauses to see how the colt reacts (b). When he sees the colt is not going to panic, he eases his other leg over the colt's back (c) and sits in the saddle (d).

the pen when he realizes the saddle is "following" him. He'll have an opportunity to get used to this once he's turned loose in the round pen.

It's usually a good idea to allow the colt time to move around while saddled, either loose in the round pen or on the longe line, before getting on his back. If he's a little skittish and cold-backed, this gives him an opportunity to buck and run, which is fine. He soon figures out that the saddle won't come off and it won't hurt him. When he stands fairly quietly and calmly, he's ready for the first ride.

For the first ride and most training sessions during the first few months, I use a plain, ⅝-inch, smooth snaffle bit. This is the same bit used with the bitting rig as described in the previous chapter.

I prefer to mount and dismount the horse for the first time with the horse tied to the wall in the round pen. Just as when I saddled him for the first time, the horse should be tied up close to the wall so he can't move around very much. I put my foot in the stirrup, pull myself halfway on and then pause to see how the horse is going to react. That way if the horse spooks, I can easily

(above and right) For the first ride, Doug turns the colt's nose to the left to prevent the colt from bucking or running out from underneath him as he gets on the colt.

step back down to the ground. When I see that he's just going to stand there, I go ahead and ease my other leg over his back.

After I get on and off the horse a couple of times while he's tied to the wall, it's time for the first ride. I begin by taking hold of one rein just a few inches from the horse's nose and turning his head to the left, which is the side I'm getting on the saddle. This control over the horse's head prevents him from bucking or running out from underneath me. Then I follow the same procedure as when the horse was tied, putting my foot in the stirrup, pulling myself halfway on and then pausing. Finally I slowly bring my other leg over the horse's back and put my foot in the other stirrup.

Once I'm on his back and the colt has a minute or two to figure out what's happened, I gradually loosen the left rein and make light contact with both reins. My objectives during these first few rides are just to teach the colt a few simple basics: to respond to my cues to walk, jog, lope, stop and back; to become used to carrying my weight while performing these gaits; and to get used to doing all of this while carrying his head and neck as close to the proper position as possible. I am not worried about speed or changing anything about his legs.

FRAMED UP

From the first step, I start asking the horse to carry his head and neck fairly close to the proper position so that his neck is almost level and his face is close to vertical with the ground. This is what I call "framed up." If his head and neck are not in this position, I ask him to drop his head down into the bridle by making light contact with his mouth and squeezing with my legs. If the horse doesn't drop his head and neck, and he probably won't during the earliest stages of his training, then I take the procedure a little further by using a direct rein to pull his head from side to side. First I pull his head to the left, for example, and hold it there until I feel him give in to the bridle. Then I release that rein and pull him around to the right and again hold it there until he stops resisting my pull. When I release both reins, his head should go back in front of his body and drop down. If it doesn't, I repeat the procedure, perhaps pulling the horse a little further around. This can be done while standing still or moving forward. Note that it is not a quick jerking procedure, but rather a firm pull.

GOING FORWARD

To ask the horse to walk, I move my hands forward, cluck to the colt and very gently bump my legs against his sides to urge him to walk. I spend several minutes walking the colt around the pen, guiding him all over the arena with zig-zag and serpentine patterns so he learns to turn. I teach the horse to guide by first laying my outside rein against his neck to push him and then using my inside rein to pull him on around in the direction I

Doug teaches the colt to guide by laying the outside rein against the colt's neck and pulling the inside rein in the direction Doug wants the colt to go.

Doug teaches the colt to back up by firmly pulling backward with both reins.

want him to go. By beginning with the outside rein and then following through with the inside rein, I teach him the concept of neck reining from the very beginning.

Once the colt is over the initial shock of having a rider on his back, I cue him to jog by bouncing my legs against his sides a little more persistently and clucking a little louder. It may take a few minutes, but he'll break into a rather fast and rough jog. I just sit quietly as I again guide him all over the pen. There is virtually no slack in the reins so I can keep him under control at this faster gait.

After trotting for a few minutes, I ask him to stop and stand. The signal to halt from any gait is to sit deep in the saddle, press down in the stirrups and say "whoa." If necessary, I also pick up on my reins to help stop him. It's extremely important for safety's sake that the horse learns how to stop when he's asked to do so. That way if something goes wrong, and inevitably it will, I know I can prevent the horse from taking off with me.

THE BACK UP

The back up can be a little confusing for the colt at first. I ask for the back with firm but gentle tugs on the reins which actually pull him backward. I begin, while the colt is standing still, by picking up on the reins to make contact with the colt's mouth. Without jerking, I gently but firmly pull backward with both reins. If he refuses to go backward, I pull his head to either the left or the right using a direct rein so that he breaks that position he's locked up in. Then it's a little easier to get him to go backward. Sometimes during that first ride you may only get one step backward out of a colt, but that's okay. Whether it's the first ride or a later one, each time the colt picks up a foot and steps backward, I release the pressure in his mouth. Then I rock him back again. I repeat this procedure until he's taken three or four steps backward, then I let him stand there and think about it a minute. After a few minutes, I ask him to back again. Following two or three sessions, most colts catch on.

For the first few days I usually spend twenty or so minutes walking and jogging, then stopping, standing and backing while using every square inch of my round pen. Everything is done quietly and patiently as the colt gets used to carrying my weight.

THE FIRST LOPE

Once the colt is reasonably quiet and responding to my cues to go forward, turn and stop, he's ready to lope. This may happen on the first day, but usually it's not until the second or third ride. The signal to lope is pressure from my outside leg against his ribs while making a "smooching" sound. The colt isn't going to step right into the lope. He's going to trot very fast around the arena for several laps while I continue smooching and bumping my outside leg against his side. I also lift the inside rein which lifts the horse's inside shoulder. This encourages him to pick up the correct lead. Eventually he will break into a lope. When he does, I let him lope only once or twice around the round pen and then ask him to halt. I then ask him to do the same in the other direction.

Throughout these early sessions I ride the colt with just enough contact with his mouth to guide him and prevent him from getting his head down between his knees to buck. I also keep the colt's head and neck in front of his body and as close to level as possible. Carrying weight is a new sensation for a colt. He's trying to figure out the easiest way to do it, so he may lift his head and hollow out his back in an attempt to make things easier. When that happens, I repeat my procedure for framing up the horse. As always, the second he corrects his head position, I release the hold on his mouth. If he gets this response every time he lifts up, he learns that he has to stay framed up. For the horse who is naturally built to do this, it is merely a matter of putting his face back where it belongs. For the horse who is not naturally inclined to do so, it means putting his head and neck back where you trained him to carry it using the bitting rig.

From the first ride, I'm thinking about getting that colt out of the round pen and into the big arena. That's my goal. Unless the colt is unusually skittish or broncy, I expect to be out in the big pen after only five or six rides in the round pen. I don't like to keep a colt in there any longer than that because going around in those little circles against a solid wall just isn't good for a pleasure horse. He isn't experiencing what it's really like to go down the rail in regard to the distractions of the surroundings and other horses. It's difficult to bend or move him around enough to teach him anything. But most importantly, while constantly moving in a small circle against the round pen wall, he won't learn how to hold himself up on a straight away. For all of these reasons and more, I want to be riding the colt out in the main arena just as soon as he's guiding fairly well between the reins and he knows to stop when I say "whoa."

7

The Big Arena

A horse's first few rides in the big arena are going to be an adjustment period. I keep him off the rail, working near the center of the pen using many different patterns and straight lines as described in this chapter. During these first rides, the horse seems to be drifting all over as he struggles with concentrating on what I'm asking him to do while also taking in all of the new sights. My goal is to get the horse to respond to my cues, whether they be to lope off, to jog in a straight line or whatever. I try to accomplish this in twenty or thirty minutes each day, and I always try to end the session on a positive note.

SUPPLING EXERCISES AND LEARNING TO TURN

I begin by suppling the horse at the walk. I do this using a direct rein and pulling the horse around in one direction. If I pull on the left rein, the horse should bend his head and neck to the left and walk in a small circle to the left. At first, the horse is slightly resistant to my pull because he is too green to automatically know that I want him to go in a small circle. As soon as I feel him give to my hand, and that usually only takes a couple of circles, I release his head and let him take a few steps to straighten back out. Then I pull his head to the opposite direction and repeat the procedure. I may do this two or three times in each direction. I use my legs to make corrections. If the horse doesn't want to go forward, I bounce both legs softly on his sides to keep him going. If he fades to one direction or the other, I use my leg to push him back over. By starting the session with this exercise, I teach him to give to the bridle while also loosening him up through the neck and the poll.

(pages 68-69) By using both a neck rein and a direct rein, Doug's horses are broke to guide either way.

(opposite) Doug guides the horse in a large arc at the walk using his left rein to tip the horse's nose toward the left and his right rein to keep the shoulder from drifting to the outside.

(below) Figure 7.1 At either the walk or the jog, I guide the horse in a large arc by using my inside rein to tip his nose in the direction I want him to go. My inside leg is pressed firmly against his side to hold his body up. My outside leg is used only if the horse drifts to the outside. These arcs teach the horse to follow his nose while holding his body up straight.

Next I spend a few minutes just walking and jogging in straight lines and large arcs (see figure 7.1). To guide the horse in a large arc, I use a direct rein to tip his nose in the direction I want him to go and use my inside leg to hold his body up. In other words, by pressing with my inside leg, I prevent him from leaning into the arc. I don't really use my outside leg, unless the horse begins to drift to the outside. Then I use my outside leg to push the shoulder back over so that it follows his neck and head in the direction of the arc. This teaches the horse to follow his nose while holding his body up straight. It also supples the horse's body as he curls around my inside leg.

While working the horse on straight lines, I occasionally pull the horse's head gently to the left and then

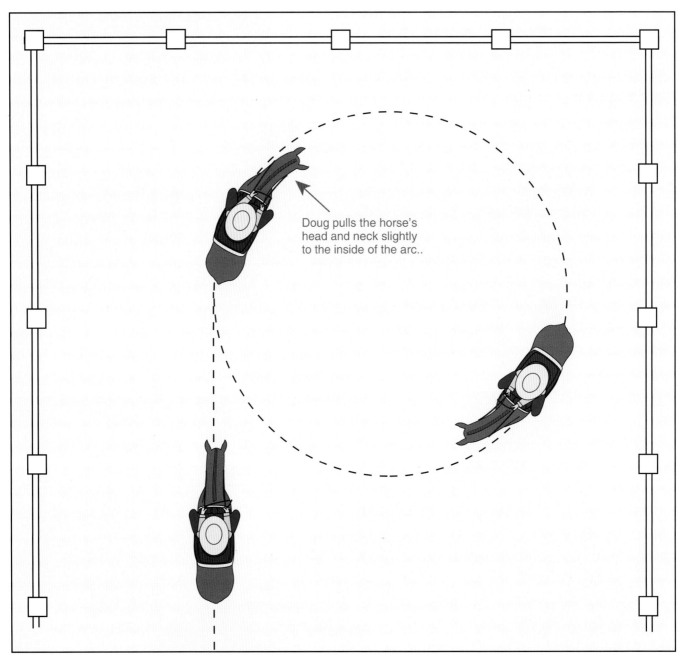

Doug pulls the horse's head and neck slightly to the inside of the arc..

(above) **Jogging on an arc teaches the horse to follow his nose while holding his body up straight.**

(right) **Doug pulls the horse's head gently from side to side to teach the horse to drop down into the bridle while suppling the horse's muscles through the neck and poll.**

(opposite) **Figure 7.2 Working in a lot of abstract patterns quickly teaches a horse to guide. I begin by jogging the horse in a straight line while on a fairly loose rein. When he starts to veer off that straight line, I turn him sharply in the other direction. Sometimes I just overcompensate in my correction by turning the horse about 90 degrees or I may pull him completely around so that he's going in the opposite direction. I first use the neck rein to ask for the turn and then follow through by pulling with the direct rein. Eventually the horse learns to guide solely off the neck rein.**

immediately back to the right and then release. This teaches the horse to drop down into the bridle while also suppling his muscles.

At the jog, I like to work the horse in serpentines and many other abstract patterns (see figure 7.2). I jog the horse in a straight line and just as soon as I feel him start to drift in one direction, I turn him sharply in the other direction. Sometimes I just overcompensate in my correction by turning the horse about 90 degrees and sometimes I pull him completely around and head in the opposite direction. In this exercise and all that follow, I use both the neck rein and the direct rein. I first ask the horse to turn by laying the outside rein against his neck and if the horse doesn't respond by turning, then I pull him in the direction I want him to go with the direct rein. Then I turn him loose, expecting him to travel in a

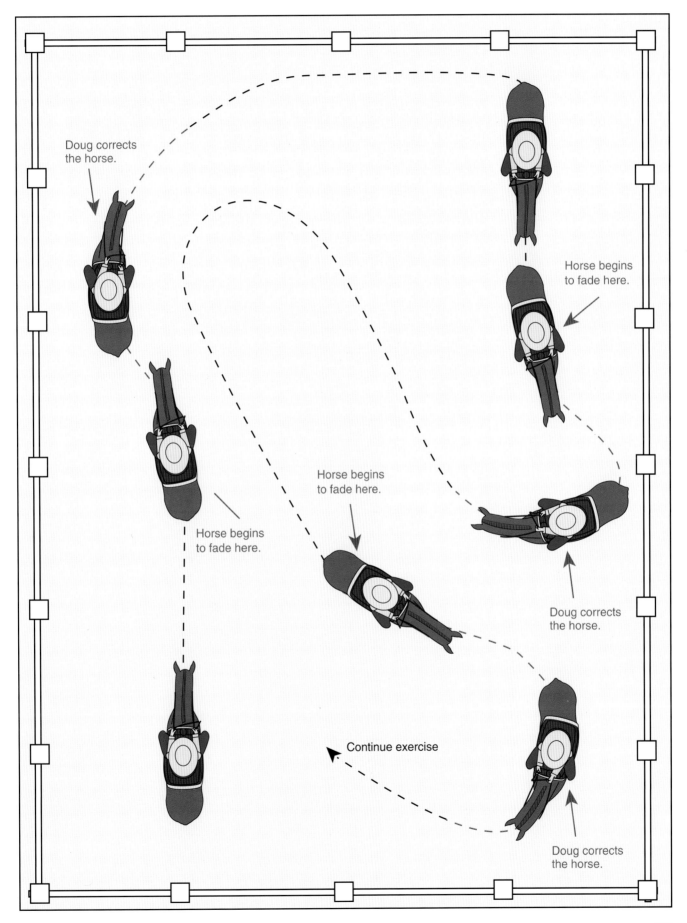

Doug corrects
the horse.

Horse begins
to fade here.

Doug corrects
the horse.

Horse begins
to fade here.

Horse begins
to fade here.

Doug corrects
the horse.

Continue exercise

Doug corrects
the horse.

(above) When the horse is properly framed up and traveling in a straight line with his head in front of his body, Doug drops his hands and jogs the horse on a loose rein.

(right) The horse's body is curved nicely around Doug's inside leg as he uses his outside rein to guide the horse in a large circle.

straight line again. He'll probably go straight for several strides, and then veer off to either the left or the right. Again, I turn him around in the opposite direction. Sometimes I just work a serpentine pattern going back and forth across the arena. As I head toward the rail, I wait to feel the horse start to make the turn on his own. As soon as he does, I pull him in the opposite direction. These exercises teach the horse to stay between the bridle reins and wait on me to tell him which way we're going next.

I maneuver the horse all over the arena, working in a lot of serpentines, circles, arcs and straight lines. This is the fastest way I know to teach a horse to guide. Since I use both a neck rein and a direct rein, my young horses are broke to guide either way, usually in just three or four days. Also, by varying my patterns so much I instill a very important concept in my program — the idea of having the horse wait on me to tell him what to do. A horse that is ridden around and around in a circle gets bored. He knows to just keep going forward, and he's probably going to get sloppy doing it because it doesn't require him to think. With my program, he has to concentrate on me because he never knows what's next.

During all of the above exercises, I use my legs to the degree that they are necessary. If the horse tends to jog very fast and turns when I ask him to, I won't use my legs much at all. If the horse is very lazy, I need to bounce my legs softly on his sides with each stride just to keep him from breaking down from a jog to a walk when I turn him. If I move the horse in an arc and he drifts to the outside, I push him back over to the inside using my outside leg. Determining how much leg pressure and when to use it depends on the horse and the situation.

At several points throughout these exercises I stop and back the horse. This varies the routine a little more. It also gets the horse comfortable with backing which is important because I use it a lot in my advanced training techniques. At this point in the horse's program, I use the same pull and release method described in Chapter 6. After I back him just three or four steps, I sometimes let the horse just stand and relax for a minute or two. The horse has a chance to catch his breath and think about things for a minute, which may prevent him from getting nervous about all the new things he's being exposed to.

At several points throughout the sessions Doug stops and backs the horse. After backing, he allows the horse to just stand and relax.

LEARNING TO LOPE

After I spend two or three days just walking, jogging, stopping, standing and backing, the horse is ready to lope in the big arena. Before asking the horse to lope for the first time, I warm up the horse using the same exercises described above.

I cue a horse to lope by taking a light hold of his face, laying my outside leg into his side and then making a "smooching" noise. For the first few times I lope the

(above) During this first loping stride, Doug lifts the inside rein to lift the horse's inside shoulder. The outside rein is held low to hold the outside shoulder in position.

(below) At the lope, the horse should drive off the hock of the outside rear leg.

horse, I guide him in a large circle near the center of the arena. The outside rein controls the horse's shoulder, so it is used as a neck rein to guide the horse in an arc. I lift the inside rein, using a direct pull, to lift the inside shoulder. At the same time, I push or kick with my outside leg. This not only sends the horse forward, it also moves his hip over slightly toward the inside. The hock of his rear drive leg is then underneath the horse, which forces him to drive off it. (For the left lead, this is the right hind leg). I want the horse to pick up his inside shoulder, shifting his weight to this hind leg and then push off that leg. If the horse fades to the inside, which many do, I lay my inside leg firmly against his side for support and use my inside rein more firmly, pulling up and over the neck to push him back out. The outside rein is held low near my thigh to hold the outside shoulder in position.

It should also be noted that many people make the mistake of leaning forward when asking the horse to lope. Don't lean forward. After reading my description of the lope departure, you can see how leaning forward naturally makes loping off even more difficult for the horse.

With the green broke horse, the standard response to the cue to lope is a few strides or even a few laps at a long-trot before the horse breaks into a lope. Be patient. Let the colt lope once or maybe twice around a large circle in the center of the arena and then bring him back

down to the walk. Let him settle, and then ask again. It depends on the individual horse, but I usually lope a green horse two or three times each direction and then go back to doing something he's more comfortable with like walking or jogging. I don't want to tire the horse physically or mentally.

It may take several weeks before a horse is comfortable loping off. I'm patient but firm with my cues. If the colt just seems lazy, I get a little more aggressive and expect him to respond more quickly. But if he's truly confused or physically weak, I give him all the time he needs to figure this out on his own.

Other than working on the departure itself, the only thing I do during the first two or three loping sessions is allow the colt to find his legs and establish his rhythm. I guide him in a big circle or a square several feet off the rail. I keep my legs down against his sides for support, and I don't regulate his speed in any way. Nor do I try to alter his movement. I keep his nose tipped slightly toward the inside of the circle with his head and neck close to level with his body.

Everything at this stage of the game is going to be fairly crude. The horse is still trying to get comfortable carrying my weight so his speed is erratic. He's still fading left and right, and he may even stumble a few times. I try to make it easy for him by sitting still in the center of the saddle. If I keep my balance, it's much easier for the horse to stay balanced.

After about a week of this type of riding, it's time to start working on improving the horse's natural ability and preparing for the show pen. My program for training a pleasure horse to walk, jog, and lope is presented in the following three chapters. The back up and transitions are discussed in Chapter 11.

"THE WALK CAN BE USED TO BENEFIT THE HORSE'S ENTIRE TRAINING PROGRAM."

8

The Walk

This chapter and the following three focus on refining a young horse's talents once that horse is green-broke. Information on the walk, jog, lope and transitions are each covered separately within their respective chapters. When training a young horse at this stage in my program, I incorporate the necessary portions of each chapter according to the individual horse's progress. For example, one horse may naturally jog well but struggles at the lope, while another horse needs very little help to be able to lope like a show horse yet requires extensive work at the jog. I suggest reading all four chapters up front, and then referring back to the sections which apply specifically to your horse as you go along.

There is no set schedule or time frame when it comes to training horses. (See also Chapter 5 regarding how to evaluate physical maturity.) At this point in my program, I ride a horse I'm training for the two-year-old futurities five or six days a week for thirty minutes to an hour each day. The horse also spends time turned out in the round pen or on the hot walker for additional exercise. My goal is to teach the horse to walk, jog, lope, back and execute transitions while using good form and maintaining a consistent speed. The horse should appear effortless to ride, so he has to do all of this on a loose rein and with minimal cues from me as the rider. This might take 90 days or it could take a year. Regardless, I continually monitor the horse's physical and mental condition and then proceed with or back off my program as needed.

THE SIMPLEST GAIT

As the old saying goes, "You have to walk before you can run." Such is the case in western pleasure, where

(pages 78-79) Teaching the horse to side-pass.

(opposite) Doug cues the horse to walk by moving his hands forward on the horse's neck and gently waving his legs against the horse's side. This horse responds by dropping his head and neck and moving off into a natural, relaxed walk.

Every training session begins with bending and suppling exercises at the walk.

the walk is the foundation for the more complicated gaits which follow. It's such a simple gait that the walk is basically judged on a pass or fail basis rather than graded on style. Yet it is mandatory. If a pleasure horse won't walk, it doesn't matter how well he jogs and lopes.

The walk is defined as a four-beat gait with each leg moving independently and with the feet touching the ground at different times. The walk is completely inherent to the horse. Other than keeping his attention focused and his speed consistent, a horse walks no differently in the show pen then he does in the pasture. Unlike the jog and the lope, the rider does not attempt to influence how the horse's legs move. Considering such, many people think the walk doesn't require much time and effort. They spend many more hours jogging and loping than they do walking.

It's true that all pleasure horses are pretty much created equal at the walk. But the walk can also be used to benefit the horse's entire training program. Because the

CHOOSING BETWEEN THE SNAFFLE BIT AND THE HACKAMORE

In the third or fourth month of training a two-year-old, I decide whether I plan to show the horse in a snaffle bit or a hackamore, also called a bosal. I try all two-year-olds in both to decide which the horse prefers. If I decide to show a particular horse in a hackamore, I incorporate this new equipment into my training program. I don't restrict my training to using just the hackamore, but I use it about fifty percent of the time so the horse is completely comfortable with it.

I determine if a horse is better suited to a snaffle bit or a hackamore according to how sensitive the horse's mouth and nose are. If the horse seems to like the bit, i.e., he doesn't chew on it and he responds appropriately to pressure from my hands, I usually show him in a snaffle. Personally, I prefer the snaffle because I feel I have more control with it than with a hackamore. The only exception to this would be if the horse is good in a snaffle but even better in a hackamore. The horse shows me this by how well he gives to my hands, how framed up he tends to stay on his own and how mellow or relaxed he seems. Usually in an instance where the horse is good in both equipment, I prepare him to be shown in either and alternate throughout the year. In some cases, however, the horse clearly does not like one or the other. The horse tells me he does not like the bit by chewing or "mouthing" it a great deal. Therefore not only is the bit less effective in the show pen, it also contributes to an unpleasant picture of the horse going down the rail because the constant chewing is distracting and the horse looks unhappy. In this case, I am better off showing the horse in a hackamore. If the horse is exceptionally dull or sensitive across the top of his nose, he's not going to do well in a hackamore. He tells me this by either not responding at all to pressure from my hands while in a hackamore or by tucking his head too much or tossing his head in irritation. Some horses never get used to a snaffle bit. Some horses never respond well to a hackamore.

The hackamore works by applying pressure to the nose and jaw, while the snaffle bit applies pressure inside the horse's mouth. Up until this point in the horse's training I've used only the snaffle bit, but the horse has a pretty good understanding that when I pick up on my reins and apply leg pressure he's supposed to drop his head and frame his body up. He also understands that when I apply neck pressure with the left rein and then follow through with direct pressure from the right rein, he should turn to the right and vice versa. This previous training makes the transition to the hackamore a fairly easy one if the horse likes the hackamore. My training techniques aren't really any different with the hackamore, I just establish the different feel of the pressure to the nose and jaw rather than the mouth.

horse is most relaxed while walking, it's a good time to teach a horse a lot of things. Bending and turning and the suppling exercises explained in Chapter 7 were introduced to the green broke colt at the walk. Once the horse understands the basic concepts, like how to move in an arc or work in the serpentine exercises I described in Chapter 7, we ask the same things of him at the jog and lope.

For the first 120 days in my training program the walk is mainly used for suppling exercises and as a time for the horse to relax. I cue the horse to walk by moving my hand or hands forward on his neck and gently waving my legs against his sides. He should move off into a natural, relaxed walk with his head and neck properly framed up. If his head and neck come up, I frame the horse back up using my reins and legs as described in the previous chapter.

Every session begins with the bending and suppling exercises described in Chapter 7. Again, this helps loosen up the horse through his poll, neck and shoulder. These exercises also get the horse thinking about me. I spend five to ten minutes at the beginning of each session with every horse I ride, no matter what age they are, walking, bending and turning. Throughout the session, I go back to the walk to allow the horse time to relax or to settle down. If the horse gets tired or frustrated from being schooled at the jog or the lope, I walk him for a few minutes to let him freshen back up physically and mentally.

VARYING SPEED AT THE WALK

Although I don't train the horse to walk during the first 120 days, I pay attention to his natural inclination to walk fast or slow. This determines when I start teaching him to walk like a show horse. If he likes to walk really fast, I may start the following techniques after only 60 or so days of riding. If the horse naturally walks very slowly, it isn't necessary to start working on this until about six weeks before the first futurity or show.

A show horse needs two gears at the walk; slow and fast. I use the slow walk to hold a good position on the rail. The fast walk is used to pass another horse and get an open position on the rail in front of the other horse. I put these two different gears in a horse by using my legs. If the horse's natural tendency is to walk slowly, as I hope it will be, I sit back in the saddle and put my weight down in the stirrups. This teaches the horse to associate feeling my weight pushing down through the stirrups with going slow. Allow the horse to walk as slowly as he wants. If you're not used to this, it can be difficult to just sit there without rushing the horse. Let the horse figure out that this is a comfort zone. The less you handle him, the more he relaxes and the slower he walks.

If the horse tends to walk fast from the beginning, you have to teach him to slow down. He must learn patience. The best way to do this is to let him take just a few steps forward. The second you feel his momentum start to build, push down in your stirrups, tell him "whoa" and make him stop and stand. He should stand there, with his head and neck in position, until you feel him relax. Then softly ask him to walk off again.

Repeat this procedure numerous times. At first you'll probably only allow the horse to take three or four steps before stopping him. Gradually, as the horse begins to figure out that he's going to stop and stand after every few steps, he starts anticipating the halt. With each step he'll be listening for your "whoa." This is exactly what

Figure 8.1 It's easy to teach a horse to side-pass by using a fence to prevent the horse from going forward. Make light contact with the horse's mouth, and lay the outside rein against the horse's neck to move the front end in the direction you want the horse to go. At the same time, move your leg on that same side back a few inches behind the girth and use it to push the hind end over. Through repetition the horse eventually learns to sidepass without the fence.

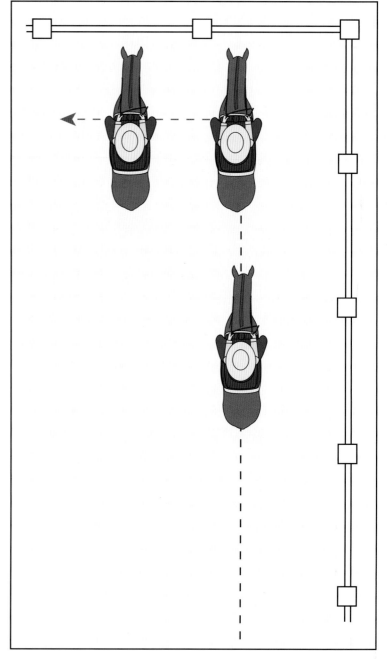

you want him to think about. Some horses quickly catch on to this concept and walk slowly after only one or two sessions. For others it is a lesson which must be repeated throughout their show career. It takes a rider's patience to teach a horse patience.

To speed the horse up, I move my hands forward on his neck, ease off the pressure in my stirrups and gently fan my legs against his sides. It's a very subtle, gentle motion meant to encourage the horse to take a little bigger step and to pick his feet up a little faster. It should not scare the horse into jumping forward. Once the horse picks up a little speed, I let him continue at this rate for several strides. I then slow him back down by sitting back in the saddle, moving my hands back to their normal position and pressing my weight down in my stirrups. The horse should come back to me and slow himself down. If he doesn't, I pick up on my reins to make contact with his mouth and ask him to stop and stand. Once he's settled, I move him off into a slow walk again. I repeat this procedure several times each day. I vary the time I spend at each speed and stop and stand often.

In some cases, if a horse isn't paying attention to me or if he's particularly aggressive at the walk, I back the horse up a few steps when I tell him "whoa." I am as aggressive as his attitude warrants. By getting after him a little bit like this, I refocus his attention on me rather than on hurrying or on anything else which might have broken his concentration. I get him thinking about what I want to do, which in this case, is stopping and standing at any moment.

SIDEPASSING

A good way to gain control over the horse's body is by working on lateral movement (see figure 8.1). This is particularly helpful at the jog, but it begins at the walk with the sidepass. Sidepassing is also useful in suppling a horse through the shoulders, neck and poll, and it encourages the horse to reach with his hind leg.

The easiest way to teach a horse to sidepass is by walking him directly toward the arena rail. The horse's body should form a 90 degree angle with the fence. Make light contact with the horse's mouth, and lay the outside rein against the horse's neck where it meets the shoulder to guide the front end. Move your leg on that same side back a few inches behind the girth and use it push the hind end over. Encouraging him to move will frustrate the horse at first since he's facing the fence and unable to go straight forward. However, the neck rein and leg pressure guide him in the one direction he can go. Through repetition, the horse learns to move laterally without the fence to prevent his forward motion. It is an exercise that serves as the foundation for the lateral movement you'll soon teach the horse at the jog.

"THE WAITING GAME"

Very early in my training program, I introduce the horse to the idea of waiting on me. This is a very important concept in western pleasure. I always want the horse thinking "wait, wait, wait." It teaches the horse patience, and it contributes greatly to what we call "stay back" which is highly desirable in a pleasure horse. Think of it like this, a good pleasure horse is technically able to walk, jog or lope slow or fast. But since a western pleasure horse is ridden for pleasure rather than to accomplish something or as a means of getting somewhere in a hurry, we want him to go slowly. It's easier and more pleasurable to ride a horse who is jogging slowly than it is to ride one that's trotting fast. Furthermore, we judge pleasure horses on their ability and grace. Moving slowly has a greater degree of difficulty.

9

The Jog

Second gear is the jog. Here the horse lifts his back and softly swings his legs, using little hock or knee action, in a precise two-beat rhythm. Cadence is critical as a hind foot and diagonal front foot hit the ground at precisely the same time. This clean, soft, sweeping, up-and-down motion is dependent on the hocks reaching well under the horse's body and the front legs reaching out in front of the body. A good jogger has a cadence reminiscent of a clock's pendulum, with the diagonal legs swinging under the body in steady rhythm.

Training a horse to jog to the best of his ability includes allowing a colt time to find his own natural rhythm, building his overall body strength by long-trotting and then evaluating his natural talent or ability at this gait. Some horses are simply born great joggers and the only thing I need to work on with them is consistent speed. If a horse is less than perfect, I evaluate his problems, use specific exercises to improve his weaknesses and then determine if his level of ability is going to keep him from being the caliber of show horse I look for. I'll talk more about that evaluation at the end of this chapter.

ASKING FOR THE JOG

It isn't difficult to get a horse to jog. From the walk, I gently bounce my legs against his sides at about the same speed as I want the horse to move his legs at the jog. I make soft but firm contact with my calves against his barrel. If the horse doesn't respond by picking up the jog, I bump my legs a little harder against his sides or for a truly dull-sided colt or an older show horse, it may be necessary to use spurs. The idea is to use my legs to

If the horse raises his head from it's proper position, Doug gently takes hold of the horse's face and uses his legs to encourage the horse to round his back and drop his head.

Doug releases his hold just as soon as the horse drops his head and neck.

(pages 86-87) A good jogger has a cadence reminscent of a clock pendulum.

encourage the horse to lift his back. In other words, I want the horse to push off his back legs by reaching under himself. This causes the back to raise slightly. At the same time, I also make a clucking noise that the horse probably already associates with jogging from his longing sessions. By clucking in the same slow, steady rhythm that I use with my legs, I ask the horse to pick up his feet and go forward into a jog.

Ideally the horse should respond by lifting his back and softly stepping into the two-beat rhythm of the jog without altering his head and neck position. If he raises his head from its proper position, I gently take hold of his face so that the horse drops back down into the bridle, just as we did at the walk. As soon as the horse responds by dropping down into the bridle, I release my contact with his mouth. If necessary in the early training stages, I take hold of the colt's face like this to steady him as I ask him to jog however he eventually needs to do all of this on a loose rein. Taking hold of the horse's face just prevents him from rolling forward into a faster walk until he eventually breaks into a jog. By "holding his face," I prevent some of the forward motion while encouraging the up and down motion with my legs.

Once the horse has changed gears and is jogging, I give him a minute or two to figure things out. I sit quietly on his back and guide him with my hands and legs. Determining how much or how little to use my leg at the jog depends on the individual horse. If the horse is resisting or not jogging well, you have to use more leg. If the horse is a crisp jogger and tends to be a little fast, use less leg.

For the first few weeks I still work the serpentine patterns, small circles and other patterns described in Chapter 7. But once the horse has learned to guide and stays between the bridle reins, meaning he doesn't drift from side to side, then I gradually spend more time working in a large circle or square about 10 feet off the rail. My priorities gradually change as the horse progresses in my program so that I eventually work on the horse's cadence and speed. I still, however, revert back to those earlier exercises if the horse shows me that he's confused or he starts making the same mistakes he made as a green broke horse. For example, if the horse is jogging down the long side of the arena and he starts veering off toward the inside of the pen, I may pull him around sharply in the opposite direction. I continue jogging this way for a few feet, and then I pull him around and head back the other way. With just that quick reminder, the horse goes back to jogging straight forward, and he waits on my cue to head in a different direction.

CONTROLLING SPEED AT THE JOG

A young horse usually starts off kind of quick at the jog, but if he has a good sense of natural cadence he soon rates himself a little bit and slows back down to a comfortable jog which won't be much different than the jog of

USING THE SPUR CORRECTLY

The spur is often a misunderstood tool of this trade. When used correctly, it is a valuable one. For our purposes, the spur is used only as an aid to moving the horse's body forward, over to the left or right, or upward as when we ask the horse to lift his back.

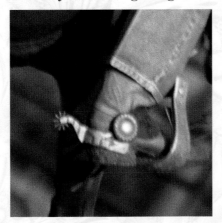

I have long legs, so I first signal the horse by using my calves. Then if I don't think I got my message across, I go to my spur. This is done by lightly poking the horse with the spur. That way the horse learns that following the signal from my calf comes the poke of the spur, and he can take action to prevent that spur. A person with shorter legs might not have that much control with his calves, but he can go to the spur to get the horse to respond.

Pay attention to how the horse responds to the spur on a daily basis. I seldom use a spur on a horse every time I ride him. I just use it to make his sides "lighter," or more responsive, and then I take the spurs off. When I sense he's getting dull to my legs again, I go back to the spur for a few days. I don't use a spur every time a ride a horse because it can become irritating to the horse.

The horse will tell you if you're using the spurs too much or too severely. If he jumps forward when you barely move your legs, you've over-spurred him. If the horse wrings his tail or pins his ears every time you touch his sides, he's probably irritated by the spur. Take the spurs off and allow the horse to learn to trust that your legs won't hurt him.

Specific types of spurs and their use are discussed further in Chapter 14. But remember that although the length of the shank and the type of rowel determine how severe the spur can be, it is the person using them who is responsible for applying that severity.

a finished show horse. However not all horses are this talented, and even the most talented joggers occasionally speed up. Erratic speed is the most common problem at the jog when preparing the horse for the show pen.

If a horse jogs too fast, either all of the time or only occasionally, I slow him down using either a small circle or by backing him up. Both exercises work well, but each horse is different so it's up to you to decide if one exercise works better than the other with your horse.

To use a circle to slow the horse down, I wait until the horse speeds up and then use a direct rein to pull him around in a fairly small circle, about 10 feet in diameter. This forces him to shorten his stride. The circle also breaks his concentration and interrupts his thoughts on going forward so the horse naturally slows down. Soon he starts to figure out that if he jogs too fast, he's going to get pulled around in this little circle. A horse can't go very fast in this tight of a circle.

I also find the back up to be very useful in teaching a horse to jog slowly, just as it helped teach him to walk slowly. When the horse starts speeding up, I first press down in my stirrups and lean back a little in the saddle. This serves as an early warning that I'm about to stop the horse, and eventually he learns to slow down when he feels me do this. I pick up on the reins making contact with his mouth to stop the horse, back him up a few steps and let him stand for a second or two. Then I put him back into the jog. If he speeds up again, I stop and back him again. At first I don't pull the horse back too severely. Generally speaking, I let the punishment fit the crime. For a young horse who just kind of drifts off, I stop him quietly and ease him back six or seven steps. Then I let him sit there for a few seconds to settle. If the horse is intentionally cheating on me or simply not trying, I may set him down a little harder and pull him backwards for 15 or 20 steps. This gets his attention and lets him know I'm not just along for the ride. Again, I pause to let him regain his composure, and then ask him to jog off again. I give the horse a little rein and trust him, but the very second I feel him start to leave or lose his cadence, I push down in my stirrups, shut him down and back him up. It doesn't take long for most horses to figure out how this works. Meanwhile, by backing the horse up, I've gathered that hind leg back up under him where it belongs.

The procedure of stopping and backing is repeated over and over until the horse catches on to the idea of "staying back" at the jog. This usually takes about a week or two. At that point, all I have to do is push down in my stirrups or pick up on my reins and the horse knows to slow himself down, which is what I eventually need him to do in the show pen. Throughout the horse's career, if I ever feel he is getting dull to the idea of staying slow at the jog or coming back to me when I pick up my reins, I always return to the back up. Even the older horses may need this reminder once or twice a day.

It should also be pointed out that backing a horse like this teaches him that when something goes wrong, we're going to stop as opposed to running forward. Therefore he'll be less likely to panic and take off if we get in a bad situation.

THE LONG TROT

The main thing a horse needs to be a good jogger is strength. With a two-year-old in particular, building body strength is usually the single most important aspect of his training. Strength comes with exercise. Long-trotting, or extending the jog, is best for strengthening the hind leg and teaching the horse to use his hind end for impulsion, thereby improving a horse's ability to jog. Once I'm into about the second or third month of training, I use it a lot in my training program.

It's important to realize that there is a big difference between extending the length of the stride and increasing speed. Trotting fast doesn't do anything but teach a horse to go forward in whatever sloppy, easy manner happens to cover the most ground. It destroys that "stay back" frame of mind we're striving for in western pleasure and teaches the horse to use quick, short strides. Properly done, however, the extended trot serves as an exercise which makes the horse use his hind leg and his shoulder to reach forward. Furthermore, when two diagonal legs spend extra time in the air reaching forward, the other two legs are therefore spending more time on the ground. In other words, I'm creating a situation in which the horse can actually remain "slow-legged" while covering far more ground.

In order to reach further under himself with his hind leg, the horse has to hold his back up. He also swings his

front leg forward clear up at the shoulder for maximum reach. All of this is hard work for a horse and is therefore excellent for conditioning and strengthening muscles. Naturally a stronger horse can jog and lope slowly more easily than a weak horse.

The theory behind long-trotting is that we're making the horse use his body rather than just pulling himself along with the front legs and dragging his hind legs. We want to make them push with the hind leg. Begin by gathering up the slack in the reins so you have light contact with the horse's mouth. This allows you to keep the horse from merely going fast in response to your leg pressure. Then, from a jog, sit deep in the saddle and use your legs to bump and squeeze the horse's sides with each stride. Each time the horse hits the ground, use both of your legs to drive the horse. I also usually begin by clucking with each stride.

I don't really want the horse to go fast, it's more of a medium long-trot. The main priority is that the horse is using himself. At first a young horse or a poorly conditioned older horse may only be able to long-trot a few laps. It's an exercise used to build endurance, so don't

The extended trot makes the horse use his hind leg and his shoulder to reach forward.

overdo it in the early sessions or the horse becomes overly tired and sore. Instead incorporate it into your daily riding sessions to gradually build up the horse's strength. I usually start my two-year-olds out long-trotting for less than five minutes each session, and gradually over the course of two or three weeks I build them up to ten minutes a day. Even with the older show horses I rarely long-trot for more than ten minutes.

EVALUATING THE JOG

After a solid thirty days of allowing a horse time to get comfortable with jogging while also building his strength through long-trotting, it's time to make an evaluation and work on a horse's problems. Each horse is an individual, but I'll begin by describing the ideal jogger and then talk about weaknesses and how I aim to make each horse a better jogger.

As I stated in the very first paragraph of this chapter, the jog is first and foremost a two-beat gait. This is mandatory. From there, I look for the horse who takes an even stride with each leg while swinging his legs with a slow, rhythmic cadence. He should pick his feet up high enough to clear the ground and then place each softly, almost delicately, on the ground. The length of stride differs according to the size of the horse, but ideally I want the hind leg to leave the ground while it's still under the horse's hip and then reach well under the horse's belly. At the same time, the opposite front leg should reach forward an equal distance. The key here is that the horse swings his legs slowly. A truly great jogger appears suspended in air as his legs slowly swing back and forth under his body. The speed is consistent and the rhythm almost monotonous. Because the horse is moving so softly and with little knee or hock action, the rider enjoys a comfortable, gentle sway from left to right with little or no jarring.

We hear a lot about a horse leaving his hocks out behind him at the jog. This stems partly from conformation and partly from training. A horse built with his hocks set out behind him is naturally more likely to leave his hind leg out behind him at the jog. It is considered undesirable for the hind leg to be left on the ground so long that the hock stays out behind the point of the hip, because this creates a strung out, long-strided jog. Also, because the horse takes an equal stride with his front legs, the horse flattens out his body further by taking a longer step up front. Eventually he is kind of pulling himself along with his front legs while dragging his back end behind him.

Whether the horse is a green broke colt who is physically built to jog this way, or an older show horse who has merely gotten lazy at the jog, I work on the problem in the same ways. First, I do a lot of long-trotting to build strength in the horse's hind end and across his back. And, as I described earlier, by holding the horse's face with my hands and driving him with my legs, I encourage impulsion from the hind leg.

With a weak jogger I take this a step further by using my hands to hold his shoulders up at the jog while encouraging impulsion from the hindquarter with my legs. This is done by clucking to the horse while holding his face with my hands very high over his shoulders. At the same time, I push him up into the bridle with my legs at a regular jog. This lifts the horse's shoulders and gets him up off that front end. By clucking to him, I encourage him to pick up his feet, but without going faster. I sit back in the saddle, like I'm showing the horse, and bounce my legs against his sides in the same rhythm as I want him to use at the jog. It's a slow, rhythmic bumping rather than the driving force I use at the long-trot. Since the horse might be inclined to go faster, I stop the horse and back him if he speeds up. Eventually he learns to associate my position in the saddle, the slow bounce of my legs and the clucking noise with framing himself up.

It's always important to remember to give and take. Don't get the horse going too "downhill" by pulling on his face so much that he just drops his head lower and lower while bringing his chin in toward his chest. I want a horse to pack his head, but I have to realize when he's over-bridled, or past vertical. Also, I can't just hang on to his face continuously. I have to be able to turn the horse loose and see what he's going to do.

Several exercises teach a horse to use himself correctly at the jog: circles, lateral movement and stopping and backing. By doing some of each, I make a horse use his body. This is not only good for a poor jogger, it also gives a good jogger something to think about. It keeps him from getting bored and lazy with just jogging on the straight line or down the rail. As always, when you make a horse work at something more difficult, that rail work seems like a reward. The horse is happy to get there, relax and do his job.

Doug uses his hands to lift the horse's shoulders while also encouraging impulsion from the hind end by bumping his legs against the horse's sides.

CIRCLES

As I described earlier in this chapter, pulling a horse around in a very tight circle is useful in teaching a horse to jog slow consistently. But slightly larger circles are also great for teaching a horse to jog correctly because the natural arc of a circle puts a horse's body in a position which encourages him to pick up his feet and use his legs properly.

For this exercise I jog the horse in a circle about 15 feet in diameter. I begin by making light contact with the mouth and using my inside rein to tip the horse's nose toward the inside of the circle. My outside rein is used as a neck rein to guide the outside shoulder. I bounce my legs against the horse's sides softly to encourage him to pick up his feet. Jogging a horse in a circle like this for five or six laps helps the horse with coordination and rhythm. After I feel the horse establish a more consistent two-beat pattern, I release my inside rein and jog him in a straight line. As soon as I feel him loose that rhythm, I go back to this circle routine.

(opposite) Figure 9.1 I teach a horse to move laterally after increasing his momentum to a working trot. With light contact with the horse's mouth, I tip the horse's nose to the inside with my inside rein and use my outside rein as a neck rein to push the outside shoulder over. My outside leg is used to push the horse's body toward the inside. As the horse progresses with this lesson, I gradually stop tilting his head toward the inside and simply push his shoulder and hip over with my outside rein and outside leg.

Circles also help correct a horse who is "flat" at the jog, meaning his stride is too long, and he is pulling himself along with his front legs rather than pushing from behind. The is usually what is happening if the horse is leaving the hocks out behind the hip, dragging his hind feet across the ground, and or carrying his head and neck excessively low. To work on this, I guide the horse in a circle but I also hold my hands high above his shoulders and really use my legs to encourage impulsion from behind as I described earlier in this chapter regarding weak joggers. Doing this while working the horse in a circle takes both techniques one step further. It forces the horse to hold his shoulders up and reach a little deeper behind. At the same time, it shortens his stride and improves his rhythm. Once I feel all of this happening, I lower my hands and bring him out of the circle.

LATERAL MOVEMENT

Moving the horse laterally, from side to side, also improves a horse's jog by encouraging the horse to use his inside hock. It starts with a diagonal type movement in which the horse's head is tilted to the side. Gradually

(above) Moving the horse laterally improves a horse's jog by encouraging the horse to use his inside hock.

(Right) With the horse's nose tipped very slightly toward the inside, Doug uses his outside leg to push the horse over laterally.

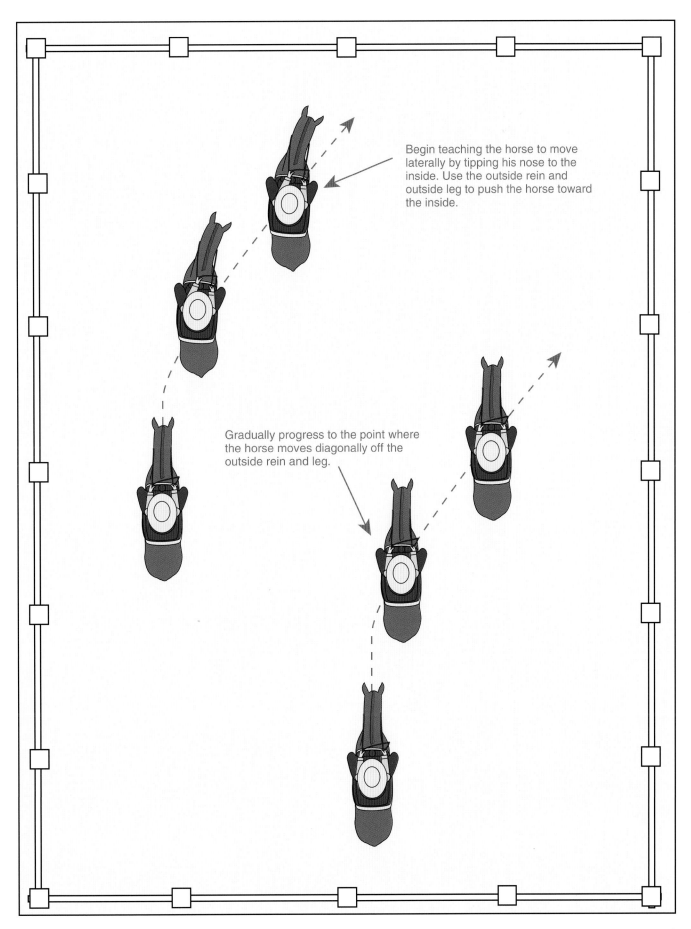

Begin teaching the horse to move laterally by tipping his nose to the inside. Use the outside rein and outside leg to push the horse toward the inside.

Gradually progress to the point where the horse moves diagonally off the outside rein and leg.

we advance to where he's moving diagonally across the arena with his head in front of his body (see figure 9.1).

Moving laterally at the jog can be done at different speeds, but generally a good working trot which is slightly longer strided than a typical western pleasure jog gives the horse the momentum he needs. I'm asking for impulsion here, so in essence we want the horse using his legs to reach over and forward. As I head across the long side of my arena at a working trot, I make light contact with the horse's mouth and move the horse toward the inside of the arena by tipping his nose very slightly toward the inside with the inside rein. My outside rein is used as a neck rein and pushes the shoulders over laterally. If necessary, the outside rein can also serve as a direct rein to prevent the horse from arcing his neck too far toward the inside as if he were going in a circle. With the head and neck in the proper position, I use my outside leg to push his body toward the inside. In other words, rather than bouncing both my legs equally against the horse's sides, I move my inside leg back a little further toward his hip and push very firmly to send him over and forward rather than just forward.

All of this causes the horse to push off his hind end and push up into the jog. Begin by asking for just a few strides diagonally across the pen, and then reward the horse by allowing him to go straight forward. Naturally some horses catch on to this concept faster than others, but most horses learn to move laterally at the trot in just two or three sessions.

Some horses find it easier to go one direction than the other, and you may have to adjust the amount of rein and or leg pressure to compensate when he is reluctant to move over. As the horse progresses, gradually stop tilting the horse's head to the inside and just rely on your outside rein to push the front end over while your outside leg pushes the hind end over. Again, move the horse laterally across the pen and then reward him by allowing him to move straight forward.

STOPPING AND BACKING

I've already discussed how to stop and back a horse to work on speed, but this is also useful in improving a horse's jog because it tends to get the back end up under the horse. Looking at the photograph here you can see that when a horse backs up, his body shifts back over his legs. His hock is pushed deep under his body. Therefore if a horse is getting strung out at the jog, I stop and back him, using the same procedure described throughout this book, to shift his body back over his hind legs where it belongs.

After backing a few steps I put him right back into a jog. Since he starts off with his hind legs well underneath his body, my goal is to encourage him to keep them under himself. Naturally, I repeat the back up and use it in combination with the other exercises I've described as often as necessary.

Backing the horse shifts his body back over his hind legs where it belongs.

A SECOND EVALUATION

Determining whether a horse is a good enough jogger depends on several factors. I look for horses to compete at the top levels of AQHA and futurity competition, so my standards are pretty high. Also, in some aspects, everything averages out. If the horse is an outstanding loper, he can get away with being a little weak at the jog. But he's got to be able to make up for his weaknesses somewhere. Some horses do it by being steady. Others are exceptionally pretty. Generally speaking however, the winners in today's competition have it all or close to it.

Furthermore, I'm also a little more inclined to forgive a weakness at any gait if the horse shows me he'll let me work on his problems. I determine this by always asking a little bit more out of a horse with each training session and then seeing how the horse reacts. Is he accepting training? Or getting mad and staying mad? If it's the latter, odds are he won't ever make a great pleasure horse.

Training certainly contributes to a horse's attitude in the arena. With this in mind, I try to ensure the horse enjoys his job by giving him time just to enjoy the exercise without schooling on him — a time when he can just be a horse. I don't want him to think that it's always a burden to be ridden. Starting in about the fourth month of riding, when I have his jog and lope under control and he's stops and steers nicely, I introduce new surroundings to the horse. I might ride him out through the pasture. Or sometimes I load him on the trailer and take him to a neighbor's arena to ride. This gives the horse a good break from the monotony of seeing the same arena every day, plus he learns to do his job in a different environment. If you have time to take the horse out on a trail ride every once in awhile, I also recommend that. Again, you're exposing the horse to new environments which help lessen the shock of seeing the sights at the first futurities or shows.

Finally, keep in mind that once you accomplish something in a session, start looking for a good place to quit. When the horse jogs nicely for 15 or 20 feet, particularly if he finds that spot on his own, I stop him real easy, in a positive way, and step down off his back. I quit on a good note, and this gives a horse self-confidence.

"A GREAT LOPER DRIVES HIS HOCK AND HIS BACK LEG CLEAR UP UNDER HIS BELLY."

10

The Lope

There's no way to overemphasize the importance of the lope in western pleasure competition. A pleasure horse's ability to lope is his single greatest attribute when he's offered for sale or being judged on the rail. That's why it's often called "the money gear."

Why is the lope of such great interest to pleasure horsemen? It's probably a combination of reasons. We're fascinated by the sensation of "galloping" a horse in slow motion, which makes it both smoother and safer for the novice rider. We recognize that it's as much a natural talent as speed is to a race horse or cow sense is to a cutter. Therefore we can improve upon or detract from it to some extent with training, but we're largely at the mercy of the talent the horse is born with. That makes every prospect a gamble and the truly great lopers worthy of our respect and admiration. It's extremely important to realize that not every horse, even those who are bred and trained to lope, can swing the hock, rock back and lay the front leg out there — slowly, softly, gracefully.

In technical terms, the lope is defined as a three-beat gait, with a slight hesitation between the first and second beat. The count begins when the rear drive foot hits the ground. Next, the off-fore and lead hind foot strike the ground almost simultaneously to make the second beat. The third beat is added when the lead foot strikes the ground. As with the walk and the jog, I must emphasize that the number of beats is mandatory, i.e., the horse is not loping if a fourth beat is added.

What makes a horse a great loper? The two most important characteristics by which I judge a horse to be a great loper are the impulsion from behind and the length of the hesitation between each stride. A great

The horse reaches full extension with his lead leg and is considered "flat-kneed."

loper drives his hock and his back leg clear up under his belly. This enables him to lift his front end off the ground and reach full extension with the lead leg before it touches the ground. Following each stride, a great loper appears to almost pause before driving that back leg forward again for the next stride. Both of these qualities contribute to the appearance that the horse is in slow motion. It should not be animated, but rather the lope should be a soft, smooth, flowing motion in which the horse appears to glide effortlessly.

To train a horse to lope to the best of his ability, I begin by mastering the lope departure as described in Chapters 7 and 11, and then allowing the horse to find his own natural rhythm. Every horse has an individual style as part of his natural ability, so I give this time to develop. Evaluations are made along the way to determine if the horse has enough ability. Then I focus on teaching the horse to allow me to rate his speed and to control his hind leg for greater impulsion and his front end to keep his shoulder from dropping. Please note that there are two very important notions regarding the lope that I can't control and therefore don't try to control. First, if a horse doesn't have the will and the ability to go slow, I can't make him do so. I'll talk about this further later in this chapter. Secondly, I'm a firm believer that if you take care of the hind leg the front leg will take care of

(pages 98-99) The "money gear."

The horse is not driving as deeply with his hind end and has "too much knee."

itself. In other words, we want a pleasure horse to keep his knee as flat as possible at the lope but the best way to do that is to make sure the horse is using his hock properly.

In my program, training at the lope includes gaining control over three things; speed, the hind end and the front end. All three are incorporated with maintaining proper head carriage. After I've loped the average horse for a week or so in the big arena, I usually introduce the draw reins to help maintain proper head carriage at the lope. Everything happens a little faster at the lope, so things can unravel and go wrong faster, too. This is particularly true with the horse's headset. Draw reins simply help keep the horse's head from coming up so fast that I can't prevent it.

They work by using a sliding mechanism to pull the head down rather than the direct pull of a regular rein. I use a smooth snaffle bit with the draw reins. They are attached on the girth rings under the stirrup leathers for horses that naturally carry their heads close to level. For a horse who carries his head exceptionally high, I attach the reins to the girth's ring under the horse's belly. I ride the horse using the draw reins two or three times a week, but I'm always evaluating the horse as to whether he needs more or less time in them. If I see that when I pull on the reins the horse's head drops entirely too far down,

Draw reins help hold the horse's body, head and neck in the correct position as the horse lopes off.

101

almost as if the horse is rolling up into a ball, it's time to take the draw reins off for a while. Ideally, I use them until the horse can and will lope off with his head down. Later, if he starts having a problem, I put them back on. I ride a few horses in draw reins for most of their careers, but for most it's just a temporary training aid. Also, it's important to note that draw reins aren't meant to be used to hold the horse constantly. I use them just like regular reins in that when I need to pull, I do so and then I immediately release.

SPEED

Just as soon as the horse is in the big arena and his departures are getting fairly smooth, I start working on the horse's speed. This usually occurs after the first week or two. In the meantime, I also note how the horse handles his speed on his own. If he tends to start off fast, but soon "rates" himself, or slows back down without my help, than I know that horse wants to go slow and just needs a little help figuring out how. If the horse starts off slow but gets faster and faster, than I know that either this horse needs a lot of work learning how to lope slowly or perhaps he can't or just doesn't want to go slow. I wait to make that final evaluation until the horse is further along in my program.

Understand that speed is not the most critical element at the lope. Style is. But don't think that speed isn't important, because it is. Not because this class is judged on which horse goes the slowest, but rather because speed is directly related to the degree of difficulty. For example, let's say two 15 hand horses both drive deeply with their hocks, are equally flat-kneed and carry their heads in a very natural level position. One horse swings his legs slowly so that he appears to be in slow motion. He's relaxed, and seems to float along effortlessly. The other horse is moving his legs twice as fast and appears to be racing around the arena. Naturally the slower horse wins. He's the better horse because it's more difficult to do what both horses are doing with their legs while going slow.

As I stated earlier, a horse has to have a certain amount of will or desire to go slow. Even though a race horse drives deeply with his hock and is flat-kneed, I can't make him into a western pleasure competitor. He wants to go fast. The pleasure horse wants to go slow. That's the first requirement.

While a pleasure horse can and will go slow on his own, it's my job to teach him how to stay consistently slow. The easiest way I know to do this is by stopping and backing which is done just like we did at the walk or the jog. If the horse starts loping too fast, I put my weight down in my stirrups and sit back in the saddle. I stop him, back him up a few steps and let him stand there for a moment. Then I lope him off again. If he speeds up again, I repeat the procedure and stop and back him again. Although my intention is not to intimidate the horse, I do want to get his attention. Therefore I am as harsh as his actions and attitude warrant.

I use this stopping and backing procedure over and over and eventually, just like at the jog, the horse learns that when I press down on my stirrups and pick up on the reins I'm about to stop him and back him up. The next step will be for him to realize that when he feels me pick up on the reins, he slows down in anticipation of me stopping him. Eventually he learns to slow down when he feels me press down on my stirrups. All of this helps the horse adopt a "stay back" frame of mind. He'll still need reminders throughout his career, so I go back to this exercise frequently.

Another way to teach a horse to slow down is by stopping the horse and turning him around in a swirling motion where the horse's hip moves out and his shoulder moves in (see figure 10.1). It's kind of a combination of a traditional rollback, where the horse is turning strictly on his hindquarters, and the small circle we use to slow the horse down at the jog. This breaks his concentration and forces him to channel his energy into something other than going forward. I begin by loping the horse in a circle about 80 feet in diameter. When I feel the horse is getting too fast, I first ask him to slow down by gently

Doug teaches the horse to slow down by stopping him and turning him around in a swirling motion.

Figure 10.1 If the horse is loping too fast while working in a large circle, I bring him to a complete halt and use my inside rein to pull his head and shoulder around in a small circle. My outside leg pushes the horse's shoulder in while my inside leg pushes his hip out. This swirling motion breaks the horse's concentration and gives him something else to think about besides going forward. After turning him around two or three times, I release the horse's face, walk him forward a few steps and then ask him to lope off again.

taking hold of his mouth with both reins. If he doesn't come back to me and continues surging forward, I bring him to a complete halt, and immediately turn him sharply back in the direction I was going. If I was loping on the left lead, for example, I turn him to the left in two or three circles which are only about five feet in diameter using the direct pull of the inside rein. I also use my outside leg to push his shoulder in and my inside leg to push his hip out. I then release the horse's face, walk him straight away for a few steps and then ask the horse to lope again. I may do this two or three times before I ever lope one complete lap on the big circle.

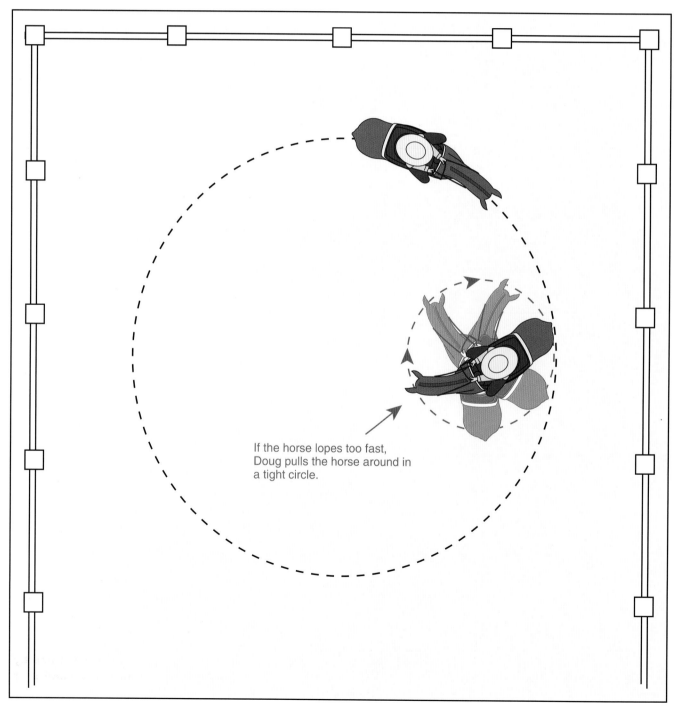

If the horse lopes too fast, Doug pulls the horse around in a tight circle.

I always try to make progress in each session, and I usually won't quit until I do. And as always, I'm looking for a good place to end my lesson on a positive note. For a horse who has a big problem with going too fast, this point may be after he's loped just a half of a lap at the nice, relaxed pace I'm striving for. When he does that, I stop him very gently and reward him by going on to something he likes to do or by quitting for the day.

There are also a few other things I can do to encourage a horse to lope slowly. In the following sections I explain how to help the horse use his legs to his best advantage by controlling the hind end and the front end. This also means that as the horse gets older, broker and naturally becomes lazier, I have to make sure he continues to work at it and lopes properly. Faster is easier, and it doesn't take long for most horses to start looking for the easiest way to do anything.

CONTROLLING THE HIND END

The hind leg, specifically the hock, is the key to understanding how a horse lopes and therefore it's also critical to how I can improve the lope through training. I start working on the horse's hind end at the lope after about a month or so of riding in the big arena. Using draw reins and a regular snaffle bit, I do this by loping the horse in a large oval off the rail. While I'm traveling on a straight line, I take a hold of the horse's mouth and lay a little outside leg on the horse to move his hip to the inside. He's still loping straight forward, but his hip is pushed over to the inside so I'm driving the inside leg up under the horse. This creates better impulsion, which is what I'm striving for. I work the horse for about five minutes in each direction, during which time I move the hip over for ten or twelve strides and then I let him straighten back out again. I don't want the horse to lope sideways for an entire lap. I just want to be able to push the hip over occasionally to strengthen that leg and increase the sweeping motion of the hind leg.

CONTROLLING THE FRONT END

As I stated earlier, I firmly believe that if you worry about the hind end of the horse, the front end will take care of itself. The front end is merely the extension of the hind end, in other words, the front legs reach out to "catch" what the hind legs drove forward.

There is one exercise, counter-cantering, that I like for strengthening a horse's body at the lope which also makes it easier for him to lift his shoulder and flatten his knee (see figure 10.2). Once the horse is four or five months into my training program and I have enough control over his body that I can easily move the horse's hip over at the lope, he's ready to counter-canter. Counter-cantering means the horse is loping on the opposite lead as the direction he is moving. For example, he is loping to the right while on the left lead. It's a difficult and rather unnatural exercise for the horse so he

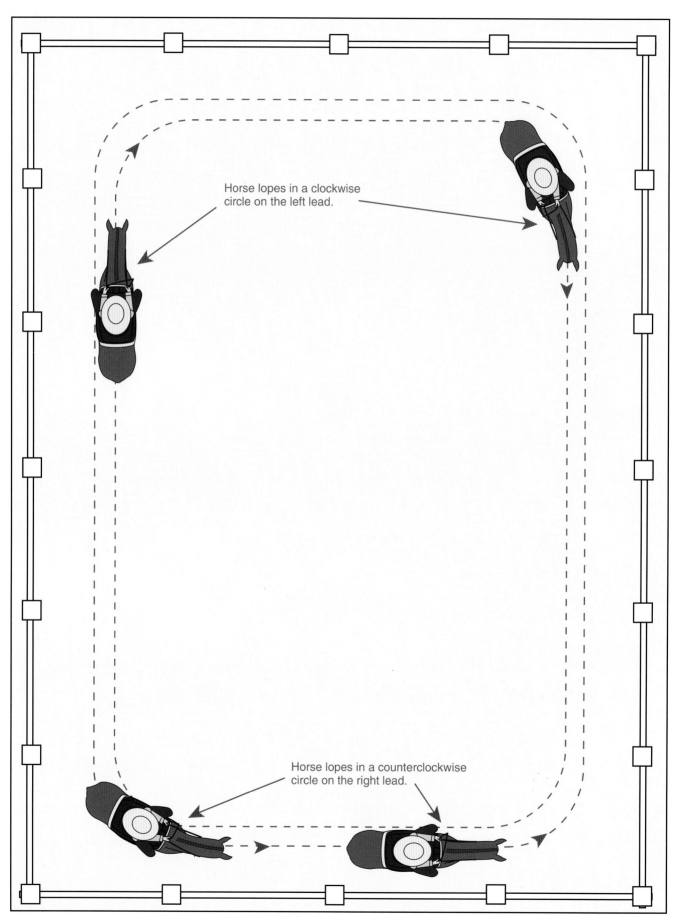

Horse lopes in a clockwise circle on the left lead.

Horse lopes in a counterclockwise circle on the right lead.

may try to break and get back on the correct lead. If he breaks, I stop him and get him back on a straight line before asking him to lope back off on the counter lead.

At the counter-canter, I use my outside hand to lift the outside shoulder, which is the lead I am on, and tip the horse's nose toward the lead leg. For example, if I am counter-cantering to the right, I am on the left lead so I raise my left hand. My other hand is held down near the saddle horn and is used simply to steady the horse through the shoulder. I use both legs to drive the horse because he is usually a little resistant and won't want to go forward. Additionally, my inside leg is pushing the horse's hip over toward the outside of the circle. This requires a lot of work on both the rider's part and the horse's. It takes patience and strength.

Because it is so stressful on a horse, I counter-canter him only two or three times a week. At first I only do it for a couple of minutes, and I gradually build up to about five minutes of counter-cantering per session. To begin, I usually counter-canter the horse one lap and then stop and reverse. Then I counter-canter him for one lap in the opposite direction. I go back and forth like that just two or three times before I quit and move on to something else. When he can do that fairly easily, I counter-canter the horse for two or three laps without stopping. Eventually, when the horse can counter-canter in both directions with ease, he is near his full potential at the lope. He's well-broke, physically strong and is highly coordinated.

THE FINAL ANALYSIS

By incorporating all of these exercises, I should end up with a horse who is loping to the best of his ability. He lopes correctly, using a true three-beat gait, and he lopes as slowly as he possibly can while maintaining that correctness. How slow can a horse possibly go? Naturally that varies from horse to horse, but it is important to realize that every horse is only physically able to do so much. I train him so that he responds to my cues. I get him physically fit so he's strong enough to use his body properly while carrying my weight. And I encourage him to drive a little deeper from behind. But the horse has a certain level of natural ability which can't be changed through training. It's our job to evaluate that natural ability, and sometimes we have to accept what we cannot change.

Counter-cantering strengthens a horse's body at the lope which also makes it easier for him to lift his shoulder and flatten his knee. Doug uses his outside hand to lift the outside shoulder. His other hand is held down near the saddle horn and is used simply to steady the horse. He uses both legs to drive the horse deep into the bridle.

(opposite) Figure 10.2 At the counter-canter the horse lopes on the opposite lead. For example, in a clockwise circle, he lopes on the left lead. I use my outside hand to lift the horse's outside shoulder and use both my legs to drive the horse forward. I also push the horse's hip toward the outside of the circle with my inside leg.

11

Transitions, Backing and the Extended Jog

For organizational purposes in this book, I include this chapter after those on the walk, jog and lope. However I work on perfecting transitions, the back up and the extended jog throughout the training process rather than waiting until the end.

TRANSITIONS

Hopefully, as this training program progresses, you come to know your horse. You find out how much athletic ability he has and how "trainable," or willing, he is mentally. This is important in how you approach your horse with whatever you are teaching him, but it's particularly helpful with transitions because it tells you how aggressive to be with your cues and what to expect in response to those cues. For example, a horse may show me that he can really lope well, both slowly and correctly, but he's a little nervous or timid. I take my time teaching him to lope off to prevent him from getting scared or mad. That way I don't risk ruining a great loper because he didn't mentally recover from the transition. On the other hand, if a horse has shown me from day one that he's just plain lazy and nothing really bothers him, I know I can get a little aggressive with him.

Regardless of how you approach a horse, the end result should be the same. The horse should appear to change gears smoothly and effortlessly. Also, his body as well as his head and neck should be in the proper position from the very first stride. I always find that if a horse starts off good, he's a lot more likely to stay good.

There isn't much more to say about going from the stop to the walk or from the walk to the jog than what I described in earlier chapters on training the horse. If you

followed the steps in my program, the horse knows to drop his head down into the bridle when you fan your legs against his sides and move your hands forward on his neck to urge him to walk. If the horse is so lazy that he doesn't normally respond by walking forward, I follow through with a light poke from my spur. The horse should jog off when I bounce my legs against his sides and cluck to him. Again, if he is a little slow or reluctant, I follow through by poking him with my spurs.

The most difficult transition for most horses is the lope off. I want the horse to push off his back legs into the lope, but their natural tendency is to pull themselves into the lope with their front legs. This is what happens when the horse long-trots into the lope, rather than going directly into the lope from the jog or the walk.

To work on this, I often use draw reins and a snaffle bit which help me hold the horse's body and his head and neck in the correct position. I don't want him to loose his frame and that can easily happen here. I start by going from the jog to the lope because I have a little more forward momentum so it's easier than loping out of a walk. I cue the horse to lope but laying my outside leg into the horse's side while using my outside rein to hold the shoulder in position and the head down. I lift my inside rein to tip the nose slightly toward the inside.

If the horse responds by long-trotting, I stop him immediately. This lets him know he's done wrong. I then back him up a step or two and roll him back over his hindquarters in the opposite direction as the way we were going (see figure 11.1). While the horse is rolling back, I have firm contact with the horse's mouth and use both hands to move the horse's shoulder in the direction of the rollback. I push with the outside rein and pull with the inside. I also really drive the horse hard with my outside leg. Then, without stopping, I firmly bump him or, if necessary, spur him with my outside leg to make the horse jump forward into a lope. If I started off trying to lope the horse off on his left lead, I stop, back, rollback to the right and then lope off on the right lead.

This rollback method is a little tricky at first, but it works because it teaches the horse to push off his hind leg. Depending on the horse's attitude, I may rollback, lope one direction for half a lap then rollback and go the other direction for half a lap and then rollback and go back in the other direction again. I don't expect a horse to catch on to this within the first lesson or maybe even the first week of lessons, but eventually he learns to lope off correctly. This same method is also used from a walk. It's an exercise I return to again and again throughout a horse's show career when I feel the horse has reverted to pulling instead of pushing off into a lope.

Any horse in my program learns early on that "whoa" means stop. It is one of the first things I teach a colt on the longe line and I continue to emphasize it after I'm on his back. Once the horse is broke and ready to show, he knows to come down from a walk, jog or a lope to a stop

(pages 108-109) Doug is aggressive with a lazy or "dull-minded" horse.

(opposite) Doug cues the horse to lope by laying his outside leg into the horse's side while using his outside rein to hold the shoulder in position and the head down. He lifts his inside rein (opposite inset) to tip the nose slightly toward the inside.

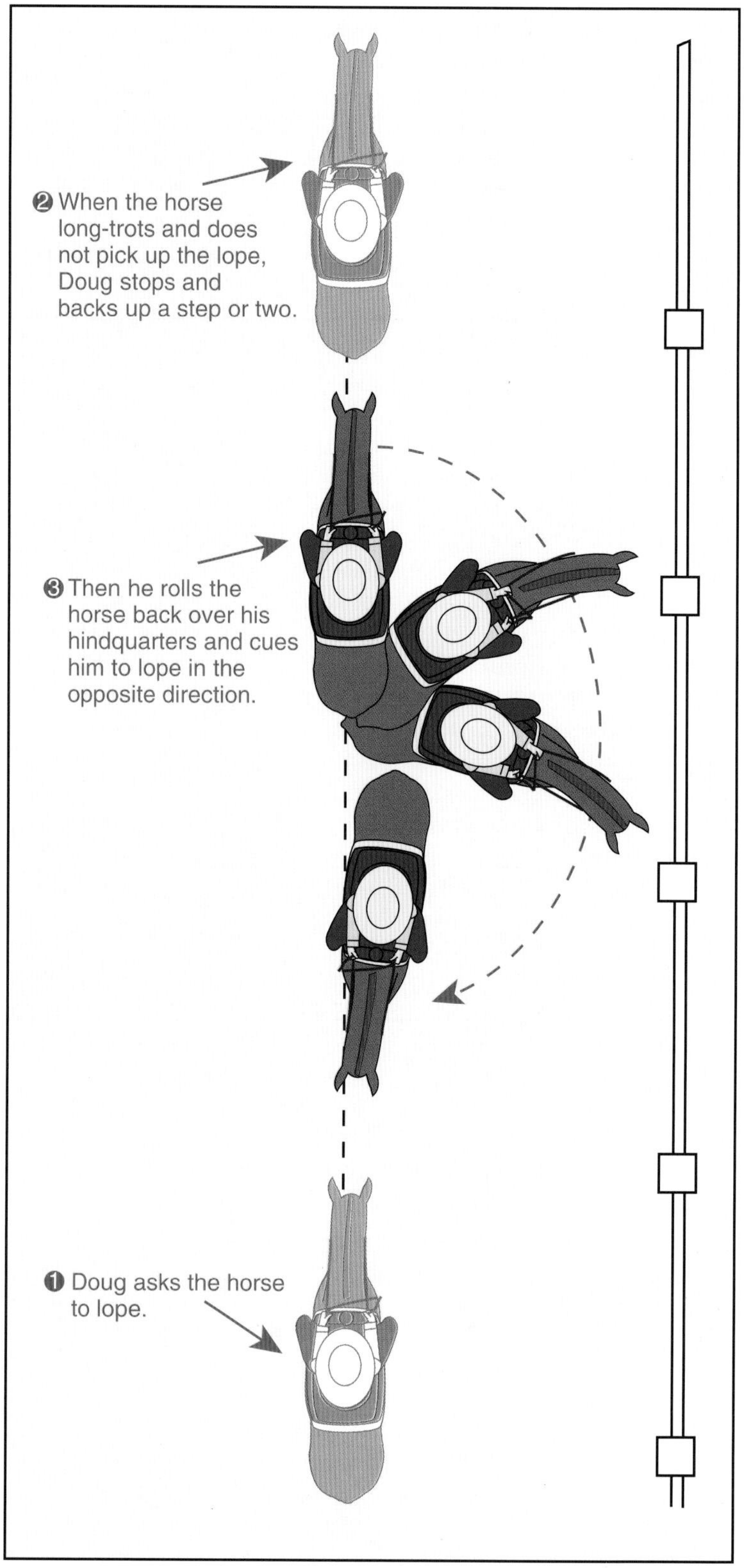

Figure 11.1 If the horse long-trots into the lope, I stop him, back him a step or two and then roll him back over his hindquarters in the opposite direction. I maintain firm contact with his mouth and use both hands to guide the horse's shoulders in the direction of the rollback. I really drive the horse hard with my outside leg while he turns around and then, without stopping, firmly bump him with my outside leg to make the horse lift up and lope off.

❷ When the horse long-trots and does not pick up the lope, Doug stops and backs up a step or two.

❸ Then he rolls the horse back over his hindquarters and cues him to lope in the opposite direction.

❶ Doug asks the horse to lope.

(opposite top) While the horse is rolling back, Doug has firm contact with the horse's mouth and uses both hands to move the horse's shoulder in the direction of the rollback. He also drives the horse with his outside leg.

(opposite bottom) Looking at the horse's hind legs in this photograph, you can see how the rollback teaches the horse to push off his hind leg.

when I push my weight down in my stirrups and say "whoa." It isn't necessary for me to use my reins at all.

To bring the horse from a lope to a walk, I say "whoa" and then immediately come back with the cue to walk by fanning my legs against his sides. This is not difficult for a horse. All it takes is practice.

Going from the lope to the jog can be a little confusing but I try to keep it simple for the horse by using my hands instead of my voice to make this transition. While the horse is loping, I pick my hands up and make contact with the horse's mouth. I pull back gently until the horse breaks into a trot. I continue to hold the horse's mouth until he comes back to the desired speed at the jog. Then I drop my hands back to their normal position at the jog.

There's no trick to making this work, it just takes practice. At first the horse may think that by picking up my hands I'm asking him to drop his head at the lope. But that cue is accompanied by my legs. When I don't use my legs, he realizes that I'm pulling him back to a slower speed rather than framing him up. After repeating this many times, I only have to pick my hands up a few inches and the horse knows to break down to a jog.

BACKING

Ideally I want a pleasure horse to back up on a loose rein by responding to my legs. But you have to realize that backing is not natural for a horse and some are very

Doug trains his horses to back up on a loose rein by responding to his legs. As the horse progresses in the program, Doug gradually uses less and less rein and more leg.

The extended jog is not necessarily as ground-covering as a true long-trot.

uncoordinated or resistant about it. Therefore I really spend a lot of time working on it, particularly with the horses who don't back well. I also think it helps that I incorporate backing into training my horses to walk, jog and lope. I back a horse so often while I'm working him at these gaits, that all I really have to do is refine my cues to have the horse backing nicely when it's called for in a class.

As I explained in Chapter 6, I start the green colts out by pulling them backward one step at a time. As they progress in the program, I gradually use less and less rein and more leg. I take a hold of their face lightly, apply my spur or my calf evenly to both sides and give the horse one slight pull to start the backward motion. Once he starts backward I release my hold on his face but I keep my legs in his sides. The horse should keep backing until I tell him "whoa." Then he stops and stands.

In the early stages of this process the horse may need an occasional pull to keep him going backward. But the key to teaching him to back on a loose rein is to release his mouth the second as he starts back. In other words, don't hang on to his mouth with a continuous pull.

Some horses back up faster than others, but speed doesn't matter to me. I'd rather that the horse back up at his own pace so he's comfortable with it and is less likely to resist. If the horse starts to move crooked, I straighten him back out by moving my hands in the same direction that his hips shifted toward. If he moved his hip over to the right, I move both hands over to the right and pull back on the reins, which moves his front end to the right and straightens him up. Moving the shoulder over is a lot faster and easier than trying to move his hip.

EXTENDED JOG

Although I long-trot my horses while training them to jog, I refine this to an extended jog, which is not necessarily as ground-covering as a true long-trot, for my purposes in the show ring. Technically speaking, a western pleasure horse is required to jog while the hunter under saddle entry is shown at the trot. Therefore, an extension of either gait is an extended jog for the western horse and a true long-trot for the English horse. Unfortunately the rules on this are vague and sometimes this gait appears to be judged according to which horse makes the most laps or goes the fastest. But for our purposes, the western pleasure horse should simply show that he can and will extend his stride at the jog and then return to the regular jog.

I begin with the horse jogging slowly on the rail. I then deliberately steer him off the rail, so that he's moving around the arena about ten feet from the rail. I ask him to extend his stride by leaning forward slightly in the saddle, making light contact with both of my legs, and moving my hands slightly up and forward on his neck. I also cluck to the horse. I start off gradually, allowing the horse to lengthen his stride a little bit at a time. In the early stages, I don't push the horse much past a medium jog. When I feel him start to scramble underneath or his head and neck come up, I know he's reached his maximum stride at that point in his training. As the horse becomes more comfortable doing this through practice, he may be able to cover a little more ground. But I don't want to push him too far so that he breaks into a lope. If he does this in the class, I am disqualified. If the horse breaks into a lope while I'm training him to extend the jog, I stop him and back him up and then start the procedure all over. I also realize my mistake in pushing the horse past his limit.

I move the horse around the arena at an extended jog for two or three laps and then I bring him back to a regular jog. To do this, I stop clucking, sit back in the saddle and release my leg pressure. At the same time, I guide him back over to the rail and then put my hands back in their normal position. At first the horse may keep jogging too fast. If he does, I stop him gently, back him up and let him settle for a minute. Then I return to jogging. Eventually he learns that when I point him towards the rail, it's time to slow down. Like everything else in his training program, the maneuver is refined through repetition.

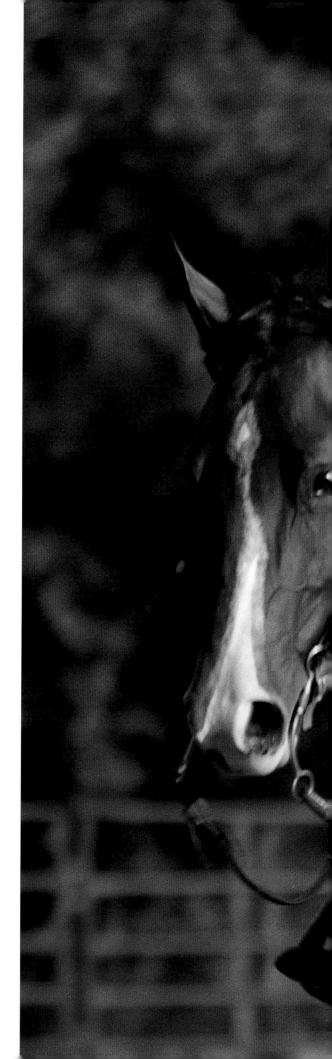

12

The Three-Year-Old

Whether you started out in my program with a yearling prospect, a finished show horse or somewhere in between, you're ready for this chapter at any point after the horse's two-year-old year. In this chapter, I give you my advice on making the transition from riding two-handed in the snaffle to one-handed in a bridle as well as how to choose an appropriate bit for your horse. I also tell you about the daily routine used for my three-year-old and older horses.

THE TWO-YEAR-OLD TURNS THREE

If I break and train a pleasure horse as a two-year-old, I usually either plan on showing him in the summer futurities which start in July and run through September, or the All American Quarter Horse Congress Futurity in October and a few later futurities through December. Both sets of horses make the transition to their three-year-old year by starting off with sixty days of complete rest. I keep them up in the stall, feeding and brushing them as if they were still on the show circuit so their haircoats stay in good shape. But I don't ride them at all. I longe them lightly two or three days a week and turn them out in the paddock for a few hours on the days in between. This rest period allows a horse time to recover from the stress of being in training. This is good for the horse mentally, but I also firmly believe that a horse develops and matures physically during this time off. It seems as if the rest period gives the horse's body an opportunity to spend it's energy on growing and developing.

When I start back riding my three-year-olds, my sessions for the first two or three weeks focus on suppling

(pages 116-117) Doug sometimes over-emphasizes his moves in order to teach the horse to push deeper into the bit.

(opposite) Making the switch from two hands to one begins by suppling the horse in the new bit, guiding him all over the pen and asking him to drop down into the bridle.

Doug likes an aluminum grazer bit, because it's light weight. He uses a half-inch chain curb strap, making sure it lays flat against the horse's chin.

and bending while also reminding the horse about the basics, like neck reining and the meaning of "whoa." I use a snaffle bit to get the horse limber using the exercises described in Chapter 7. They also remind him to give to my hands. These sessions are slow, quiet work periods as the horse gradually builds back to being at the physical and mental level he was at before his time off. I also work on getting his strength back by long-trotting and counter-cantering, but I keep in mind that it takes a few weeks for the horse to build his endurance to the level it was at when I quit on him two months ago.

SWITCHING TO ONE HAND

When the horse seems to remember most of what he learned as a two-year-old and he's supple and strong, he's ready to make the transition from the snaffle bit to a bit with a shank and a solid mouthpiece. This is simply referred to as a bridle bit. I find that this transition is extremely easy for most horses primarily because we get them so well-broke to show in a snaffle bit or a bosal. It's usually easier to ride a horse one-handed in a bridle because he respects this heavier, solid bit more.

It should also be mentioned that determining when to put a horse into a bridle bit isn't really as simple and clear cut as waiting until the horse turns three-years-old. As I mention in Chapter 14 on Tack and Equipment, I occasionally use another bit other than a smooth snaffle in the later stages of a horse's two-year-old year if I think the horse needs it. For example, if the horse is very dull in the mouth and my pull isn't getting enough response, I ride him in an aluminum grazing bit for a few days to lighten his mouth. But I ride him with two hands, and I return to the snaffle just as quickly as possible. My advice in this chapter refers to the point when the horse is ready to go to a bridle bit with the rider using one hand on a regular basis for both training and showing purposes. Even then I may go back to using two hands with a regular snaffle for a day or so if a milder bit is required for the training methods I'm using or if the horse is getting overly sensitive to the bridle. But generally speaking, I have graduated to using one hand at this point.

My two favorite bits when I start riding with one hand are an aluminum grazer and a colt correction bit. The aluminum grazer is very light weight and therefore works best on the horse with a soft mouth. The colt correction bit is made of steel and has a broken mouthpiece like a snaffle, but has shanks like a grazing bit. For the horse with a harder mouth, I try the colt correction bit. Both bits should fit in the horse's mouth so that they sit in the corner of the mouth without forming any wrinkles. I use a half-inch chain curb strap, making sure it lays flat, rather than twisted, against the horse's chin. It should fit loosely enough so that I can get two fingers in between it and the horse's chin.

The best way to decide if a horse likes a certain bit is just to go ride him in it. I start off by going through the

suppling movements of pulling the horse from side to side and asking him to drop his head and neck down into the bridle. I guide him all over the pen, at first using two hands but occasionally experimenting with one hand. I work the horse on straight lines and see how well he stays between the reins. If the horse responds well to all of this, I know I've made the right choice. On the other hand, if the horse responds to my hands by pulling away rather than dropping down into the bit, he probably needs a steel bit like the colt correction bit. If the horse tends to "wander" or move his head and neck from side to side too much, he may do better in a solid mouthpiece like the grazing bit. There are a few other bits I like, but particularly in the early stages, these are the two I use 99 percent of the time. Further description of some other bits I use is given in Chapter 14 on Tack and Equipment.

Besides telling me whether he's comfortable in the bit I've selected, my evaluation of the horse in the bridle also tells me where his weaknesses are in regard to his training. If his head and neck come up the moment I put him on a loose rein, I need to supple him more and perhaps go back to the snaffle and draw reins to "capture" his head and neck a little better. After a week or so of riding in draw reins, I try the regular bit again. I also may need to over-emphasize my moves in order to teach the horse to push deeper into the bit. This is done by pulling the horse a little further back and pushing a little harder with my legs than I normally do. I want to teach the horse to stay back off the bridle in order to keep him framed up as I've described throughout this book.

Keep in mind, too, that selecting a bit has as much to do with the rider's hands as it does with the horse's mouth. If a rider is heavy handed, in other words he tends to pull hard and often, he can and should ride a horse in a much lighter bit than someone with light hands.

ADVANCED TRAINING

Once the horse has learned the basics and has graduated to the bridle, my training objectives are simply to get the horse as broke as possible. The bridle horse is expected to perform all transitions and gaits while keeping his frame with virtually invisible cues from the rider. The only way to do this is through plenty of practice.

My daily training sessions with a three-year-old or older horse begin with a brief supling session to warm up the horse. Then I either put him on the rail or work in a large circle about ten feet off the rail and begin walking, jogging and loping in random order and for varying lengths of time. The key is to trust the horse while testing him. In other words, I put him on a loose rein and ask him to perform a specific task. For example, I ask him to lope. I trust him by putting him on a loose rein, sitting back and riding him as if I were showing him. If he lopes along nice and slow with his body in the proper frame, then I stop him gently when I'm ready and move

on to something else. If he lopes nicely for a few strides and then speeds up, I immediately take a hold of his mouth, stop him and back him. I let him settle for a moment or so, and then lope him off again on a loose rein. My purpose is to allow the horse to make a mistake and then correct it. This is much more effective in training a horse than schooling on him with every stride and thereby preventing a mistake. When you get in the show pen, you have to turn the horse loose. I'm a lot better prepared for that if I know what the horse will do when he's turned loose. Furthermore, the horse learns that as long as he's moving correctly and he's framed up properly, he's in a safe zone.

Once I put the horse in a bridle and get him as broke as possible, my focus shifts toward maintenance, preparing for specific competitions and keeping the horse mentally fresh. Maintenance is merely riding the horse; getting him out and working on his weaknesses as described throughout these training chapters. I usually go to a show at least once every six weeks, so for most of the year my riding program is geared around my show schedule as described in Chapter 13 - Preparing for Competition. If I'm not showing a particular horse for several months, however, I don't train on the horse every day. I may only ride him two or three times a week and turn him out in a paddock for exercise on the other days. This keeps the horse mentally fresh, which makes everything easier and more enjoyable for both me and the horse.

13

Preparing for Competition

The secret to success in western pleasure competition is having the brokest horse in the pen. A broke horse is one who demonstrates his abilities with little or no aid from the rider's hands and without regard to conditions surrounding him. This horse is usually the winner. Yes, it's a class judged on movement, but it won't matter how well your horse jogs and lopes if he isn't broke enough to perform in a horse show environment. For example, let's say a judge is watching two nice horses jog down the rail. The first horse is just a little long-strided and drags his toes slightly, but he's steady. The second horse is technically perfect with his legs, but he's constantly raising his head and looking off outside the arena. The rider keeps trying to recapture the horse's attention through the bridle, but eventually the horse sees something which startles him, and he shies off the rail. The first horse keeps jogging without even noticing the disruption. The first horse, despite being a lesser mover, wins.

Either early in the training process or once the horse has mastered the basics of walking, jogging and loping, he must learn how to handle two things in order to be properly prepared for competition: different surroundings and other horses.

A NEW ENVIRONMENT

Usually surroundings don't bother a pleasure horse much. The first time an inexperienced, or "green," two-year-old is hauled to a show he may whinny a few times or seem nervous about certain obstacles like metal bleachers or the concession stand for example, but after an hour or maybe even a day, he'll settle in fine. The

(pages 122-123) What really makes or breaks a performance is recovery time. If another horse flips his tail in your horse's face and scares or distracts him, you want your horse to return to performing well as quickly as possible.

secret, of course, is arriving on the grounds in plenty of time for your horse to get used to a new place. With young horses at the major futurities, this usually means at least a day before the classes begin. The more often a horse is hauled to new places the less traumatic those places tend to be, so I suggest taking a horse who tends to be nervous to friends' arenas or nearby stables as often as possible.

One exception to my general theory that horses readily accept their new surroundings is the indoor arena. We see this at the major shows and futurities which usually take place inside a coliseum or indoor arena. Some horses, even older, seasoned veterans, are nervous in these buildings. At the Quarter Horse Congress for example, trainers prepare their horses for the sights and sounds of the indoor arenas by riding in these arenas at night after the daily events are completed. For trainers with several horses, this often means staying up all night training and then showing all day for two solid weeks. It's necessary in order for the horses to be comfortable with the surroundings.

The best way to help a horse overcome his fear of an indoor pen is to show him there's nothing to be afraid of. Make sure the horse has been longed or ridden outside long enough to work off any excess energy. Try to introduce him to the indoor pen at a time when other pleasure horses are in there working quietly. It won't help matters if you have to contend with unruly timed event horses or pleasure drivers pulling carts. It usually helps a nervous horse to walk in the coliseum beside or behind a calm and quiet horse. Spend plenty of time walking, stopping and standing. By doing so, the horse will develop a relaxed attitude about this new environment.

As I stated earlier, the horse show surroundings won't present a problem for most horses. For those few who are extremely nervous when they arrive at the show grounds, I give them plenty of time to work off excess energy on the longe line and then proceed with my usual riding program to prepare them to be shown. Eventually a horse forgets about being at a new place when he gets his mind back on his job.

"TRAFFIC"

As for the other horses your horse will encounter in the show pen, often called "traffic," the best preparation is to simulate show conditions at home. This can be done by getting friends or neighbors over to ride with you or by hauling your horse to their place for an afternoon. Most people, even trainers, normally ride alone. Yet by doing so, you allow yourself to think in terms of protecting your horse from traffic problems rather than learning to deal with them. In the show ring, you won't always be able to protect your horse because when other horses and riders are involved a great deal of what happens around you is beyond your control. You have to be accustomed to working through traffic situations.

Everyone eventually finds himself riding in the middle of a pack of horses—often called a "traffic jam."

What really makes or breaks a performance is recovery time. The quicker you can get out of a jam and have your horse back moving properly, the less chance there is for the judge to see anything which gives him a negative impression of your horse. For example, let's say that while passing your horse at the lope, another horse flips his tail in your horse's face, scaring or distracting him so that he breaks down out of a lope. It isn't highly likely that the judge was watching your horse during the brief moment in which the mishap occurred, but as you make another lap around the arena you probably will make a pass in front of the judge. If your horse is loping quietly again, the judge will never know your horse broke gait. However, if he's loping with quick, choppy strides and his head and neck are up and arched unnaturally, the judge sees something is wrong. The judge doesn't know what went wrong, and he doesn't know whose fault it was, but he recognizes that your horse is in trouble.

This period, when the rider is getting the horse out of a bad situation and back to his job on the rail, is considered recovery time. Generally speaking, I shoot for being able to get out of a jam and recover within three seconds. For your horse to recover that fast, he must trust you when you tell him everything is okay. He also shouldn't be afraid that you'll punish him when something out of the ordinary happens, such as a wreck with another horse. But in order to get his trust, you must first train yourself to handle these situations properly. This isn't easy, but simulating show conditions at home helps you because it gives you an opportunity to practice handling many different situations which may come up in a real pleasure class.

Before getting into specific situations, there are a few general benefits worth taking advantage of when using this idea of simulating show conditions. First, whenever possible I suggest getting someone to stand in the center of the arena and act out the judge's role. You'll be amazed at how much different it is to ride your horse with someone watching and evaluating you. It suddenly makes you very aware of just how much or how little you're really helping your horse. This helps you make an honest evaluation of how broke the horse really is. Having someone pretending to be a judge also gives a young horse the chance to get used to a person standing in the middle of the arena.

Secondly, as you ride with other horses practice paying attention not only to what is in front of your horse, but also what is going on behind him. Showing a horse in a pleasure class is a lot like driving a car through traffic. You have to be aware of everyone around you in order to avoid wrecks and maneuver efficiently.

The following situations are commonly experienced in competition. By setting them up at home, you practice responding correctly and recovering quickly. The purpose isn't necessarily to get your horse accustomed to anything and everything, although it will make him a little less sensitive to the traffic. Instead, you're teaching him to trust you to handle and guide him so that he can concentrate on his job of moving correctly. The final product should be a broke horse and a competent showman.

TRAFFIC JAMS

No matter how well you jockey for good rail position, everyone eventually finds himself riding in the middle of a pack of horses. Prepare for this situation when you're simulating show conditions at home by deliberately putting two or three horses directly beside, in front of and behind your horse. The additional traffic may initially be distracting to you and your horse, but try to concentrate on keeping your horse steady. This is an excellent opportunity to teach your horse to depend on you to guide him safely and quietly. If you've always ridden alone, it may take your horse a few of these mock bunch-ups before he can maintain his concentration and his normal cadence and rhythm, but that's what these sessions are for. Generally speaking, it's best to just continue riding normally, expecting his best performance and complete concentration. The following section specifically covers how to handle a horse who gets faster when near other horses.

RATING SPEED

Throughout the breaking and training process, I teach the horse to "rate his speed." By that I mean he maintains the steady, cadenced way of going that I've determined is ideal for this particular horse. In the show pen, I want that horse to be able to comfortably settle in at this pace and then stay there. If a situation occurs in which he speeds up, as he is more apt to do in the show pen environment than he is at home where he was trained on a daily basis, I hope the horse will rate himself almost immediately. In other words, he'll slow himself back down. If he doesn't automatically do this on his own, I remind him to so. I recommend using the posts along the rail to help judge how fast you're going at the jog and lope. In your arena at home or in the show pen, you can easily see these "markers" as they go by and it's obvious if you pick up speed.

Although you feel your horse is trained to jog and lope correctly and therefore he'll maintain a proper speed, it's important to practice this. As with everything required of the horse, it's much easier for him to pay attention if he's the only horse in the pen. It's also easier for you to concentrate. But once you've spent adequate time training your horse, practice rating his speed with other horses in the pen.

The most common problem you'll encounter is usually that your horse wants to alter his speed according to the other horses around him. And you may find you're not as sure how fast or slow the horse is moving when you have another horse or horses nearby. This has a lot to do with getting used to the other horses in general, which just takes time and consistent riding, but if the horse consistently reacts to other horses by hurrying to catch up with them or eagerly rushing by them as if he hopes to win a race, your practice sessions with other horses are the perfect chance to break these bad habits.

As in a real class, all the horses should travel in the same direction and at the same gait. Sit back and really pretend you're in the show pen, riding your horse on a loose rein. In order for this exercise to work, he's got have the same level of communication from you now that he will in the show pen, so don't hold him back or continually train on him. Sit back and trust him. If you're using the rail posts as guides, watch them out of the corner of your eye to see how fast they're going by at the jog and the lope.

The second you see that your horse is picking up speed, stop him and back him up. Of course it's important that another horse is not directly behind you so you don't risk another horse running into you. After standing quietly for a moment or two while the other horses continue to jog or lope by, put him back in gear and again trust him to stay back. Eventually the horse will learn to maintain the speed you established in training and he'll figure out that surging forward doesn't get him anywhere.

(above series) Doug guides his horse around a slower horse and back to the rail while being careful not to come too close to the horse he's passing.

PASSING

While you want your horse to maintain that slow steadiness, you shouldn't be afraid to pass and you should practice passing in your simulated show conditions. The secret to passing effectively is planning ahead. Know where you're going before you leave the rail. Be sure not to cut someone else off and most importantly, pass with authority. This last point is discussed further in Chapter 16 on Pleasure Class Showmanship, but since it's important to practice correctly I'm going to reemphasize here how important it is to sit up and look like you're in charge. You be the one to decide when to pass, and then convey that message to the judge and your horse by riding with confidence.

Practice passing in corners and on straight-aways. In the show pen, it's ideal to pass in a corner because you have less ground to cover to get around the slower horse and can therefore get back to the rail more quickly. But that won't always be possible in an actual class. Regardless of where you pass, size up the situation early and act accordingly. Don't wait until your horse's nose is right on another horse's tail to come off the rail. Just as importantly, know when to go back to the rail to avoid putting your horse's tail in the other horse's face.

THE FINAL TOUCH

About two weeks before a horse show, I put a horse in what I call "a holding pattern." That is where I have the horse physically and mentally prepared for competi-

tion and my daily training program revolves around keeping him prepared at that level. Hopefully the horse has peaked, or reached his full potential, at that point in his training. I ride him every day to keep his energy level down and keep him highly tuned. It's also a good time to take him to a few other places, like friends' arenas, to work on the exercises described in this chapter.

By the time the horse show gets here, I want the horse to be prepared to the best of my ability. I show him and then, if the show schedule allows, I give him a week or maybe even two of rest. Sometimes I may have to keep a horse in my holding pattern for a month or six weeks during the busiest part of show season, but as soon as possible I give him a vacation between the shows. During this time I longe him lightly or turn him out for free exercise daily, but I usually don't ride him. Just like any athlete, a horse cannot remain at his peak indefinitely. I always find that trying to keep one there too long causes problems, like lameness or a sour attitude. It's like the horse has no where else to go but down. But by intentionally allowing the horse a little "down time," I provide him with a physical and mental rest period that may make the horse a better athlete next time around.

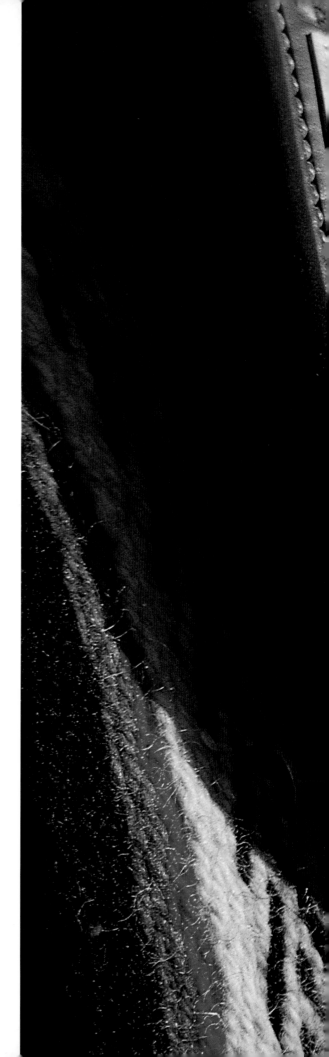

14

Tack and Equipment

Tack and equipment are a horseman's tools of the trade as well as his mode of communication. An inappropriate bit or poorly fitting saddle, for example, is comparable to a broken telephone. Both are useless in getting a message conveyed. Furthermore, if the equipment causes the horse pain or discomfort it can be mentally and physically harmful to the horse. Therefore the first thing a horseman has to demand and recognize in his equipment is that it fits the individual horse properly.

Personal preference weighs heavily in choosing equipment for any event, but it seems particularly so in western pleasure where fashion trends are more prevalent than in cutting or reining for example. The amount of silver on our saddles and bridles is always a big issue for pleasure horse riders. Personally, I don't care how much silver I have on my equipment just so long as it's of an exceptionally high quality, and it's clean when I go in the show pen.

In this chapter I discuss the functions of different pieces of equipment and tell you my specific likes and dislikes. It is up to you to find equipment properly suited to your horse and which satisfies your individual tastes.

SADDLE

Unlike cutting, which demands a saddle built to help the rider handle the hard stops and quick turns, there aren't too many specific requirements for a western pleasure saddle. I use the same saddle for both my pleasure horses and my reiners because it satisfies my basic needs when riding any horse; it puts me to close the horse for better feel and allows me to use my legs effectively.

Doug's custom-made show saddles are built so he can feel the horse underneath him.

Doug's saddles are pared out under the stirrup fenders to allow his legs to be close to the horse.

(pages 130-131) Doug likes a modest amount of silver on his show saddles to compliment the horse, yet not detract from the big picture.

The lower I am to the horse's back the better I like it. I want to be able to feel the horse underneath me. I therefore don't want the seat padded heavily or built up high in the front. A lot of people think that helps them sit up properly or keeps them from leaning forward, but it's better to put your weight in your stirrups and really ride your horse rather than just sitting there. I also don't like a saddle to be built up high in the front because it forces you to sit back against the cantle. For the sake of balance, I think it's best to sit in the middle of the saddle.

My saddles are pared out under the stirrup fenders to allow my legs to be close to the horse. The fenders are set slightly forward because I keep a lot of weight in my stirrups and want that weight based out in front of me for balance. My stirrup fenders are jointed to give me a lot of mobility with my legs. This is the opposite of the saddles used by many amateurs which are rigid in their fenders to prevent the riders legs from moving unnecessarily. Whether it's a work saddle or a show saddle, I want to be able to get to the horse's shoulder or well behind his girth. To do that I have to be able to move my legs.

Usually the less a saddle weighs the more workable it is. Thirty-five to forty pounds is best. That makes it easier on the horse and goes along with my theory regarding getting close to the horse because the lack of extra material between me and the horse insures the saddle weighs less. A lighter saddle is also easier on men when moving it from place to place or saddling and unsaddling horses.

A saddle has to fit the rider. A petite, young girl doesn't need the same saddle as a tall, heavy man. I ride in a 16-inch seat, but the best way to gauge whether a saddle is the size you need is to ride in it and see if it's comfortable. Some people like a little more room in the seat or around the thigh. Others want to feel more securely confined.

The saddle also has to fit the horse. Naturally horses vary in size and shape too, so the same saddle won't always fit every horse. Most non-pros only have one or two saddles, but then they also have only one or two horses. It's most important to make sure your saddle doesn't hurt your horse. The saddle shouldn't ride too far forward on his back or be too tight across his wither. If it does, it may rub sores on his withers or interfere with his shoulder movement. If at any time your horse seems sore-backed, it's always wise to suspect the saddle may be causing the problem.

A lot of good custom saddle makers can satisfy your personal requirements and give you a good saddle at a reasonable price. That's what most people want out of a saddle, but I also consider a saddle to be an investment. This requires exceptionally high quality and virtually no depreciation over time. Personally, I buy saddles from a highly respected saddle maker in Oregon, Don Leson. He does not mass produce his saddles and therefore they're hard to get, but I like the quality and how well they hold their value.

STIRRUPS

I put a lot of my weight on my feet when riding so the shape of my stirrups is important to me. I like "bell bottom" shaped stirrups that are narrow at the top and flare out to about 2½ inches at the bottoms. They are flat across the bottom, which gives me more support than oxbow stirrups. I don't care whether they're silver, leather or laminated wood as that mostly relates to looks and personal style. I just want them to be comfortable and functional.

SADDLE PADS OR BLANKETS

I like a thick saddle pad that dries out quickly. My work pads are usually made from a blend of sixty percent cotton and forty percent polyester. Many times I'll use two pads, for extra cushioning for the horse's back. For show pads, I use a good one hundred percent wool, hand-made Navajo show pad with a thick, soft liner pad commonly called a "felt" underneath it. (The felt pad is technically made from a 100 percent polyester fiber). The show pad is important only for looks, but that felt pad underneath is critical. I never want a show horse to be uncomfortable because the pad against his back is hard or abrasive. The good felt pads don't get this way, even after being soaked with sweat and then drying out.

HEAD STALL

Choosing a head stall is largely based on what style looks good on an individual horse, but I personally prefer one with a brow band or an ear piece as well as a throat latch strap to keep it sitting on the horse's head squarely. I don't want the bridle slipping back and forth on the horse's head when I pull his head around. This is my primary concern when choosing either a work head stall or one to show in.

Beyond being functional, a show head stall should also contribute to a horse's appearance in the pen. I am more likely to choose a head stall with silver on it for a horse with a pretty head if he consistently carries it well. On the other hand, if my horse is prone to bobbing his head at the lope or maybe carries it a notch too high or too low, the last thing I want to do is draw more attention to his head and neck. For that horse I'll choose a plain head stall to help camouflage his faults.

BITS

Choosing a bit depends on the horse and what I'm trying to accomplish at a particular point in his training. Different horses are sensitive in different parts of their mouths and since bits work by putting pressure on either the tongue, the bars (areas of lower jaw devoid of teeth), the roof of the mouth, the curb strap area or a combination of these areas, you have to decide what works best in individual circumstances. This is a broad and difficult subject, and I cannot teach you all there is to know about bits within this chapter, but I'll tell you about a few of my favorites and what I use them for in training and showing my horse. I also suggest reading the section on equipment in NSBA's Official Handbook. It provides a simple but thorough description of the equipment approved for use by NSBA. Its rules are considered standard within the industry.

A ⅝-inch, O-ring, smooth snaffle is best for starting a young horse because its jointed mouthpiece makes it a mild bit. With a snaffle the rider pulls directly on the horse's mouth rather than using the leverage of a shank. For these first few rides, I want this contact in order to guide the horse. With a snaffle I can easily pull the horse left or right, which can come in handy with a skittish colt. By pulling one rein, I've got him going in small circles and back under my control before there's time for the situation to get out of hand. A simple smooth snaffle with copper inlays in the mouthpiece and two and a half to three inch rings is a standard bit for a colt's first few rides.

This same smooth snaffle is also useful throughout my training program. It works well on young horses or even older, broker horses with sensitive mouths, especially if I'm doing a lot of pulling from left to right. Again, it gives me direct contact with the mouth.

I use a couple other bits which a horse, particularly one with a tough mouth, is more likely to respect. By that I mean the horse willingly gives to pressure from my hands through the reins, rather than leaning on the bit and consequently my hands. I don't hesitate to go to one of these bits, even with the two-year-olds. some people might think this is harsh, but a bit is only as tough as the hands which control it. Properly used, a bit with a rigid mouthpiece and the leverage of a shank is often better for the horse because the rider pulls on the horse's mouth less often. If I can pull on the horse one time and get my message across, that horse is much happier than if I'm pulling on him every few strides. This is true in training, and it becomes especially relevant in the show pen. Again, it's important to keep in mind that the bit is only a mode of communication from your hands to the horse's mouth. Therefore the rider determines the severity, as well as the effectiveness, of any bit.

I use a thin, twisted wire bit on a horse who is a little tough in the mouth, but who still needs the direct contact of a snaffle. I can use this bit for a few days and soften the horse in his mouth, particularly around the corners of his mouth, and then go back to a smooth snaffle. The horse is then more sensitive and the milder bit has more effect. There is such a thing as over-using a twisted wire, which defeats its purpose. I always want to go back to the smooth snaffle before the horse's mouth becomes raw at the corners or he is so sensitive to the bit that I can't take a hold of him at all.

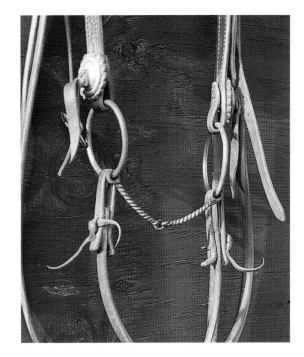

(above) Doug uses a thin, twisted wire bit on a horse that is a little tough in the mouth but that still needs the direct contact of a snaffle.

(below left) A colt correction bit has a low, jointed port and jointed shanks.

(below) A leather nose band prevents a horse from opening his mouth to escape the bit's pressure or from forming a nervous habit of mouthing the bit.

A colt correction bit has a low, jointed port, and jointed shanks. I often use it after a horse is broke into the snaffle because while it basically works the same as a snaffle, the short shanks give me a little leverage. It's a good bit for finishing a horse in because he breaks over in the poll a little easier in this bit. With a young horse that I'm showing in a snaffle, I'll often go back and forth between the snaffle and the colt correction bit to keep him responsive to my hands It's also a good bit for warming up a futurity horse at the show or using on a three-year-old as I convert him to being ridden one-handed.

In my training program I also often use a solid leather nose band placed above the bit's mouthpiece on a horse who opens his mouth to escape the bit's pressure or on one who mouths the bit as a nervous habit. It should not fit so tightly as to seal the mouth shut because the horse may panic if he gets in an uncomfortable situation. Furthermore, a nose band which fits too tightly can create a bad habit because once you take the nose band off, the horse opens his mouth worse than ever. A good rule of thumb is to adjust the nose band so you can put two fingers between it and the horse's nose. That way the horse can open his mouth a half inch or so.

Pleasure horses are often trained in different bits than they're shown in, so I'll go over the bits I show in as well. I show most of my two-and three-year olds in snaffle bits as opposed to bosals (covered later in this chapter) because I think a snaffle gives me better feel and control. There are not a lot of choices to make in picking a show snaffle because NSBA rules specify that the bit must be a "smooth snaffle with a broken mouth-piece (conventional O-ring, egg butt, or D-ring) with ring no larger than 4 inches and no smaller than 2 inches. From the cheek to one inch in from the cheek must be a minimum $\frac{3}{8}$-inches diameter with a gradual decrease to the center of the snaffle." I like engraving on the silver rings to give the bit a fancy, dressy look.

For the older horses shown in a bridle, I like to use an aluminum grazing bit, a Klapper or an A-bit. It's most important to show a horse in a bit in which he is extremely comfortable. This makes quite a difference in the overall impression a pleasure horse makes going down the rail. It isn't enough just to know the horse responds well in a certain bit. I make sure he looks good in that bit by watching someone else walk, jog and lope my horse in the show bit I've chosen before I go in the pen. The horse should not look intimidated or over-bridled (meaning his face is flexed past vertical giving the appearance of having his chin tucked to this chest) nor should his nose be pushed out too far in from of vertical. My second priority in choosing a show bit is to be able to get a lot of reaction out of it with minimal movement from my hand.

An aluminum grazing bit with a medium port is a good average bit for a horse with a light mouth. It's com-

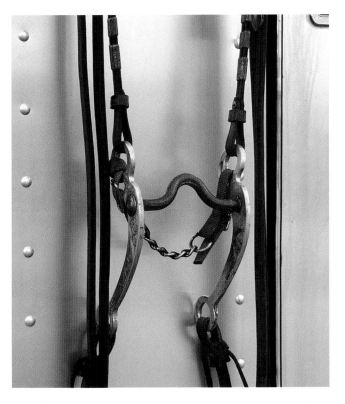

monly used on pleasure horses because the average horse tends to be very comfortable in this bit.

I like a Klapper bit for most older horses. Its medium port and heavier weight tends to give it a little more substance and effectiveness than a grazer, yet a horse still carries his head and neck out in from of him in this bit without becoming overdone.

A short A-bit has a moderate port of about two and one-half inches. I use this bit a great deal in showing a horse, and sometimes even in training one, because it works on the roof of the mouth. Unlike a more severe cathedral, however, the A-bit's lower port doesn't exert a great deal of palate pressure. I like it because it keeps a horse square between the reins and seems to get them to respect a bit more. I find this bit works well on a horse who is stiff in the poll or one who has gotten a little dull in grazing bit. When I go back to the grazer, the horse respects it a lot more. I also use it on a horse I'm likely to get into a battle with because he won't become scared of it as easily as he will a bit that works on the bars of the mouth.

(above left) An aluminum grazing bit with a medium port.

(above right) A Klapper bit's medium port and heavier weight give it a little more substance and effectiveness than a grazing bit.

CHIN OR CURB STRAP

A curb strap is technically considered optional with a snaffle bit. I always use one with a snaffle, however, because I consider it to be very necessary in keeping the bit from moving too far back and forth in the horse's mouth as I pull his head left or right. I want a snaffle to sit in place on the horse's tongue where it's supposed to be. With a snaffle, the curb strap should hang loosely under the chin, but without interfering with the horse's lower lip. It must be attached below the reins.

In a regular bit, the curb or chin strap is mandatory. I use a half inch chain chin strap, making sure it lays flat, rather than twisted, against the horse's chin. Its purpose is to enforce the bit's effect, thereby keeping the horse from leaning into the bit. It should fit tightly enough to take effect after the bit has acted on the horse's mouth but not so tightly that it grabs the chin before then.

HACKAMORES

Rather than using a smooth snaffle for a colt's first few rides, some people start off with a sidepull. It has a soft, thin rawhide noseband with rings on the sides to attach reins and a soft rope chin strap. Personally, I prefer beginning with a snaffle because it offers more control. The hide on a horse's nose and jaw are much less sensitive than the inside of his mouth. If he really wants to, a colt can pull away from me in a sidepull. But unless he happens to clench the bit in his teeth, he can't do this in a snaffle. The only exception to my preference for snaffles is if I think a horse has an extremely sensitive mouth, and I don't want to risk any trauma while guiding him during his first couple of rides. In that case, I begin with sidepull.

I do most of my training with a bit rather than a hackamore, also called a bosal, because I have more control with a bit. It's therefore easier to teach the horse how to use his body properly. But since two-and three-year-old futurity horses must be shown in either a snaffle bit or a bosal, I must decide which piece of equipment is best suited for my futurity horses to be shown in and then prepare accordingly. I ride a lot of my horses in both, switching between the two according to what the horse goes best in at a particular point in his training.

If I decide to show a horse in a bosal, I begin by schooling the horse in a steel hackamore wrapped in cotton and vet wrap. Because it is fairly heavy and unbending, it teaches a horse to give to the hackamore using the same principle as a heavier bit, i.e., the horse respects the equipment so I'm not constantly pulling on his face.

I also want this training hackamore to scratch up the skin just enough to form scabs, and then small calluses, on the horse's nose and jaw. This is necessary because otherwise the show hackamore inevitably rubs the horse's face raw. It is a violation of NSBA rules to show a horse with raw places on his face, and a horse with these tender spots tends to toss his head, or even rear, in frustration from the pain. It's unfortunate that even the softest hackamores create this problem, but the trainer can minimize the damages by toughening the horse's skin prior to the show and then allowing plenty of time for the skin to heal. I also suggest applying Vaseline or Corona to the horse's nose and jaw at the show to keep the skin supple.

The other training device I use in preparing a horse to show in a hackamore is the easy-stop, also called a

(opposite) Doug schools a horse in a steel hackamore wrapped in cotton and vet wrap.

139

The easy-stop, or quick-stop, has a nylon rope noseband which exerts pressure on the nose and a device under the jaw that acts like a "thumb" to push up on the jaw so it works using a squeezing effect on both the nose and the jaw.

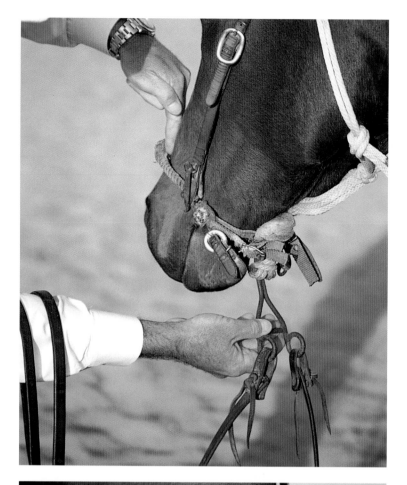

This show bosal is made from kangaroo hide, however it can still scratch a horse's face, because the skin there is so sensitive.

quick-stop. It has a nylon rope noseband which exerts pressure on the nose and a device under the jaw that acts like a "thumb" to push up on the jaw so it works using a squeezing effect on both the nose and the jaw. It is a little more aggressive than steel hackamore, and I use it on the horse who is dull to the hackamore.

The bosals I show in are expensive because they're made form kangaroo hide. Kangaroo is softer and less likely to scratch the horse's face than rawhide. I choose a specific bosal for a horse according to the size and the weight needed to match the horse's level of sensitivity. A soft, delicate, light-weight hackamore is appropriate for a horse with a small, tender nose. A thicker, heavier hackamore belongs on a horse with less respect or less sensitivity.

Most futurity events abide by NSBA rules, which state the bosal must be "no more than ¾-inch in diameter at the cheek; must be a minimum of a 1-finger space (approximately ¾-inch) between the bosal and the nose; and absolutely no metal under the jaw or on the nose band in connection with the bosal."

REINS

The reins on my training bridles are only about one-half inch wide, because I think the narrow reins are easier to handle. I can use my hands more efficiently with these thin reins. In the show pen, I go to a heavier, thicker rein which is about three-fourths of an inch wide. They look good in the show pen because they hang with a nice, smooth drape, and they are less likely to swing back and forth as the horse lopes. In training, I'm concerned with function. In showing, I'm thinking about appearance. With any set of reins, I prefer both sides of the leather to have a smooth finish because sweat from the horse's neck makes rough leather too abrasive.

I also use draw reins in my training program when I need help controlling a horse's head and neck position. These thin, round reins use a sliding mechanism which helps draw the horse's head down when I pull on the reins. The key to using draw reins effectively is a quick release, so I use only high quality draw reins which operate smoothly and efficiently. Cheaply made draw reins tend to slide slowly and are therefore counter-productive. On a horse who tends to carry his head too high, I attach the reins by either going around the horse's shoulders and then behind his front legs to the center ring on the girth. For the more average horse, I attach the reins to the rings on the ends of the girth under the stirrup leathers on the horse's sides.

With hackamore reins, called the mecate, I use only the finest horse hair reins which are made from mane hair. They're softer on my hands and the horse's neck. Thickness is a personal choice; if you have small hands you may be more comfortable holding thin reins and most men prefer heavier thick reins. As with bridle reins, the heavier they are the less they tend to swing. Color is

also a factor. If I know I can show a horse on a very loose rein and he doesn't bob his head much at the lope, I may show that off by using reins in a color which is contrasting to my horse's color. For example, white reins on a dark bay horse. If, on the other hand, I don't want to draw attention to my reins, I would use dark brown or black reins on the bay horse. Beyond that, the color is purely personal preference. Before showing a horse in a hackamore, it's helpful to stiffen the reins by wetting them. This helps keep them from swinging with the horse's motion and generally makes them hang with a nice, smooth drape. About an hour or so before the class, I wet my reins by briefly dunking them in a bucket of water going all the way to the knot but without getting any part of the bosal itself wet. Then I hook them over a door or a nail or something so they can dry while hanging with about the same drape as they will on the horse.

MARTINGALES

I often use a running, Y-fork maringale with a snaffle bit. It is adjusted to a length where it does not actually work to pull the horse's head down, but rather is there to prevent the horse from raising his head above the acceptable level. In other words, I want a direct pull from my hands to the snaffle but the martingale is there to catch the horse's head if it starts to get away from me. A martingale is particularly helpful when I teach the horse to lope off. I normally start with draw reins, but if the horse tends to put his head too low in them, I switch to a martingale.

SPURS

I use two different spurs because I think a horse becomes dull to the same rowel. I most often use Klapper spurs with ten point rowels. Then, on occasion, I switch to rock grinders to get the horse a little more attentive to my leg. I don't like to use them too often however, because the sharper spurs tend to create more tail movement.

PROTECTIVE BOOTS

Western pleasure horses are not as prone to leg injury as reiners or cutters, but it's still a good idea to use splint boots to protect the horse's legs when doing anything other than just walking. A horse I'm schooling does a lot of lateral movement as well as stopping, backing and turning. They're prone to banging their legs in these movements and besides risking injury, they also become timid or nervous if they associate moving with hurting themselves. I've often seen horses quit jogging well if they repeatedly bump their legs against each other.

(opposite) Because this mare carries her head high due to her conformation, Doug runs the draw reins through her front legs (inset). This aids in training by bringing her head and neck down when Doug pulls on the reins.

15

Tips on Shoeing the Pleasure Horse

I asked Danny Terry, who is probably the most respected farrier in the pleasure horse industry, to put into words what he thinks we should all know about pleasure horse's feet. We agree that comfort is priority number one. "With a reiner, certain shoes help him slide further. We shoe a halter horse to enhance appearance and camouflage defects in conformation. With the pleasure horses, my job is simply to make sure they're comfortable. This allows a horse to walk, jog and lope slowly because if he's comfortable on his feet, he naturally leaves them on the ground longer. I just try to make it easy for a pleasure horse to do what he's bred to do," Danny explains. The following tips are bits of advice he says everybody should know about their pleasure horse's feet.

In order to function properly, a horse's foot has to expand when it strikes the ground and the horse's weight is applied. A good farrier makes that expansion possible by using a rasp, a file used to trim the foot, to open the heels. As the horse's caretaker, you can make a significant difference by keeping your horse's feet moist. A dry hoof cracks and chips. A healthy, moist hoof expands upon impact with the ground. Daily treatment with a good moisturizer is so important.

Pleasure horse people are mostly concerned with two things: keeping their horses flat-kneed and good-hocked. In Danny's opinion, the two most beneficial things a blacksmith can do in these areas are to make sure the horse is comfortable and to not allow too much "toe" left on the horse's foot when trimming it. Several of the topics discussed in this chapter relate to comfort, but the most elementary approach is in making sure each foot

(above) This foot is trimmed short and shod level. The hairline is an equal distance from the ground on both sides of the foot.

(above right) The horse is shod at the same angle as the pastern.

(pages 144-145) A properly prepared shoe puts the pressure of the horse's weight on the outside rim of the foot rather than on the sole.

lands flat on the ground and that the horse is shod level and at the proper angle. A good blacksmith levels the foot in shoeing it, but the person caring for the horse on a daily basis should also be aware of this. Looking at the foot from the front or the back, the hairline should be an equal distance from the ground on both sides of the foot. If it's not level, one side of the hoof is going to receive too much concussion. This is not only uncomfortable for the horse, in some cases it can even cause lameness higher up in the leg as a result of the twisting action the foot develops when it breaks over somewhere other than the natural place at the front of the hoof. Study the horse's feet carefully just after he's shod and check them periodically over the following weeks. Some horses need to be shod more frequently than others just to keep their feet level.

There is no standard angle at which to shoe a pleasure horse, but Danny normally suggests that the horse be shod at the same angle as the pastern as shown in the photograph here. Your blacksmith makes this determination using his trained eye and specific tools, and we can't really teach this within the scope of this chapter. But Danny says anybody can determine if a horse's feet are shod at a comfortable angle by feeling the two major ligaments — the superficial flexor and the suspensory — halfway between the knee and the ankle. Both should feel equally dense, i.e., neither is excessively tight, which indicates strain. If the suspensory is hard and the superficial flexor is soft, the horse is standing up too much. If the superficial flexor is hard and the suspensory is soft, the horse is too low. It's not a terribly difficult diagnosis to make, but it does require some practice.

As far as length of toe, Danny believes in trimming a horse's feet as short as possible. He thinks this directly relates to keeping a pleasure horse's knee flat at the lope because the less hoof there is in front of the bony column, the less the knee has to come up for the foot to clear the ground. Generally speaking, he says he never leaves more than 3¼ inches on a grown horse, and some two-year-olds or other small horses can even go to 2¾ inches. Of course cutting a horse's foot too short also causes soreness, so it's critical not to take off an excessive amount of foot. He just advocates trimming away the unnecessary length.

Along the same line, he also thinks most horses can be helped by squaring off the toes on the back feet to safely back up the breakover point on the front of the hoof without ruining the hoof wall. This in turn helps make it possible for the hock to swing forward rather

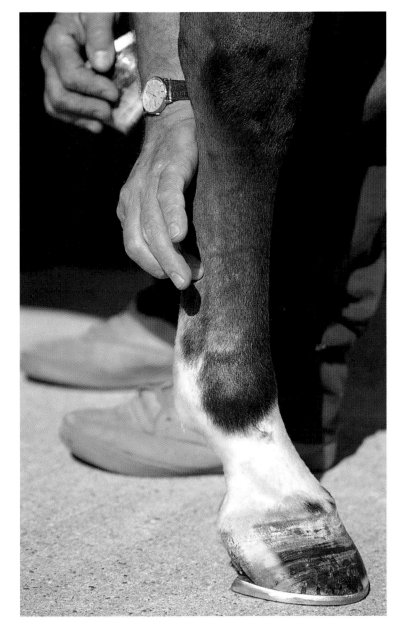

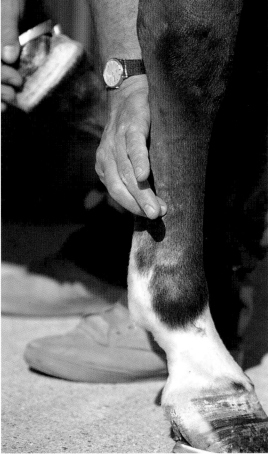

To determine if the horse is shod at a comfortable angle, Danny feels the two major ligaments in the horse's leg halfway between the knee and the ankle. Begin by lifting the opposite leg so the horse is standing with his weight on the leg being checked. Neither the superficial flexor tendon(left) nor the suspensory tendon(above) should feel excessively tight, which indicates strain.

147

The toe on the back foot is squared off to safely back up the breakover point on the hoof without ruining the hoof wall.

than having to come up and then forward. The latter creates undesirable movement in a pleasure horse's hock and is also more stressful to that joint. Danny says he probably squares off the hind feet of 95 percent of the horses he shoes.

Don't confuse small with short. One of the worst things you can do to a horse's feet is inhibit them from expanding by using a shoe that is too small. A blacksmith can and should do two things to help a horse have a larger foot that functions correctly: open up the heels and put a large enough shoe on. Danny suggests using a long shoe, one that extends about a half inch beyond the heel, to encourage this spreading of the foot and give the horse added support. Obviously the support makes it easier for a horse to go slowly comfortably. He also points out that the shoes must be properly prepared, as shown in photographs here, so the pressure of the horse's weight is kept on the outside rim of the foot rather than on the sole.

At one point in time, using aluminum shoes on a pleasure horse's front feet became a popular trend because we believed the lighter weight would make a pleasure horse flatter in his knee. But because they are so soft, aluminum shoes have to be thicker than the ultra-light steel shoes. Today, many of us believe that what you gain in the light weight of an aluminum shoe, you loose in it being so thick. It goes back to the theory of keeping a pleasure horse's foot short so the knee doesn't have to come up as high for the foot to clear the ground. The average aluminum shoes is almost ½ inch thick, and that adds length to the foot. Therefore, on the

A shoe that extends about a half inch beyond the heel helps the foot expand when it strikes the ground. It also gives the horse added support.

front feet Danny usually prefers to use a steel shoe with an ultra-light rim which is relatively thin, weighs very little and offers adequate support.

For the hind legs, he often recommends a flat steel shoe because it doesn't "bite," or grab, the ground as much. This is important because quite often the hind leg twists as the horse lopes. If the foot doesn't move, the torque going up the leg through the ankle, hock and stifle can cause serious injury.

Sometimes with the flat steel shoe, however, the hind feet tend to slip, which appears as a flipping of the back ankles. This is unattractive and undesirable in a pleasure horse, so if it occurs he suggests switching to the same type of ultra-light rim steel shoes used on the front feet. The rim causes them to hold the ground just a little more, but not as much as an aluminum shoe. In the near future many problems like this may be solved as titanium shoes become readily available. They promise to be as light as aluminum shoes and as hard as steel ones.

Finally, as simple as it may sound, remember that a pleasure horse is shod to go down the rail; to help him move his best in the show pen. Don't expect a pleasure horse's shoes to be suitable to other events or even for being turned out in the pen or a pasture. Doing so only risks injuring your horse. If you're going to turn him out where he may run and buck, protect his legs with polo wraps or splint boots. And just as importantly, use bell boots to prevent shoes from being accidentally ripped off, particularly if the shoes on his front feet extend beyond the heels as Danny recommends.

No two horse's feet are exactly alike, so many horses require special handling other than what is described here. This is just basic advice that both Danny and I think anybody with a pleasure horse ought to know because the horse's feet are first and foremost on the list of what affects his ability and attitude in the show pen.

16

Pleasure Class Showmanship

Up to this point, we focused on training the pleasure horse. This chapter is about showing one. It's important because no matter how well the horses perform, the outcome of every pleasure class is in some way affected by the rider's abilities to present the horse's abilities to the judge.

It's called showmanship, and it's mainly about professionalism in both appearance and attitude. Your horse not only has to be the best mover, he has to look like the winner. And you have to look like you know you're riding the winner. It's not too difficult when you're having a really good ride. But when conditions are less than perfect, that's when the true showmen really stand out. It's also how they'll beat you time and time again in pleasure horse competition.

The topics in this chapter cover specific ways in which the rider can improve his chances of winning without necessarily altering the way the horse moves. I've divided it into two sections. The first part covers the preparation that takes place before the class begins including grooming and the rider's mental preparation. The second half describes the rider's responsibilities on the rail.

GROOMING

One way in which we present a more polished, pretty picture is in the grooming of our pleasure horses. Every horse under my guidance goes in the show pen clean, clipped, brushed and banded.

It begins at home where daily grooming, routine worming and a proper diet ensure the horse has a short, slick hair coat. I feed my horses plain, whole oats and

(pages 150-151) Keith Whistle and Doug were first and second in the Two-Year-Old Snaffle Bit Western Pleasure at the 1991 World Show on TNT Fluid Fred and Cuiton, both trained by Doug.

Bermuda grass hay twice a day. If I want a horse to gain some extra weight, I also give him a flake of Alfalfa hay in the afternoon. My veterinarian routinely worms my show horses every 60 or 90 days.

All of the horses in my barn go through the same grooming procedure whether they are on my show string or green broke two-year-olds. Every day either I or one of my assistants brush each horse thoroughly with a standard, rubber curry comb. We start at the top of the neck and go back to the base of the tail using firm, circular strokes. The longer you curry a horse the better, so we take our time doing this. Once or twice a week we also vacuum them using a vacuum cleaner designed for horses. Like the currying, this loosens dirt and flaky skin. It also brings the oil in a haircoat to the surface. We finish brushing by going back over the horse's head and entire body with a soft body brush to whisk away any loose hair or dirt. Then we comb through the mane and forelock to remove shavings and help train the mane to lie down against the horse's neck.

A long, thick tail is visually important for a pleasure horse because it contributes to the balanced look and helps camouflage less than perfect hocks at the jog or the lope. To keep a tail as long and healthy as possible, we wash and condition our horses tails once a week. After they dry, we carefully comb or brush through the hair to remove any remaining tangles or shavings and then braid the tail. The braid keeps the ends of the tail up off the ground and prevents it from being stepped on by the horse as he backs up or rises from laying down in the stall. I also make sure there is nothing in the horse's stall like a cracked feed tub, bucket hangers or a loose nail in the wall, on which the horse could snag his tail.

On the day before the show, the horse is clipped. If the show lasts longer than three days, I re-clip about every third day. Clipping begins by first washing the horse's legs and allowing them time to dry. I clip the legs with the grain of the hair using a 10 or 15 blade because they don't clip too closely. Depending on how much hair the horse has on his legs, I usually start at about the knee and go down the back of the leg using light, even strokes. I don't want the hair to look chopped off or shaved to the skin. I just remove any long, shaggy strands. On white legs, I clip lightly over the entire white area, still using light, downward strokes with the grain of the hair. I finish the leg by using a 40 blade along the coronet band.

To clip the horse's head, I usually start at the nose and work up to the ears using 30 or 40 blades for a closer shave. I clip all of the whiskers and long hair around the muzzle including the lips, chin and just inside the nostrils. I also clip the whiskers above and below each eye taking care not to cut the eyelashes. Before starting on the face and jaw, I remove the halter and fasten it around the horse's neck so it's easier to maneuver the clippers. Going with the grain of the hair and using light,

BANDING A MANE

First wash the mane with soap but no conditioner. If the mane is clean and already dry, use a squirt bottle with water to dampen it. Damp hair is easier to work with and it usually lies flatter if it dries after it's banded. It's best to use a fine-toothed, men's hair comb to part the hair, making sure the part is straight. The hair you are not working with yet may be held back out of the way with the comb or a ladies "alligator clip." It's usually best to make anywhere from four to eight wraps. A thick mane naturally needs fewer wraps than a thinner one. Each consecutive wrap of the band should lie underneath the other. This creates a more uniform appearance and helps the mane lie flat against the horse's neck.

Starting at the top of the mane, gather a section of hair about a half-inch wide.

Hold the section of hair you're banding between your right forefinger and your thumb. With the rubber band in your left hand, wrap around the section of hair.

Pull the band to the side rather than up every time you go around the hair.

Pulling down on the hair while you twist the rubber band for the next wrap also helps the band lie flat.

The bands should lie flat against the horse's neck and be uniform in size.

Sometimes pulling very slightly helps slide the rubber band up a little tighter against the base of the neck.

153

even strokes, I clip the bottom of the jaw, in between the jaw bones and down to the chin.

Once I finish the face and jaw, I slip the halter back on the horse and, if necessary, use a twitch to clip the horse's ears. If the horse stands still without a twitch, that's fine. But most horses don't like to have their ears handled and there is less of a fight if I just put the twitch on to start with. The horse's ears are clipped on the inside going downward into the ear. On the outside, I turn the clippers over and lightly brush the edge of the blade over the ear while going with the grain of the hair. I finish by clipping around the edge of each ear.

The bridle path is clipped using a 40 blade. I start at the point where the poll starts to drop on the horse's forehead and go back down the horse's neck following the general rule of thumb which suggests clipping no further back than the length of the ear.

On the day of the show, the horse is bathed if conditions permit. I won't give a horse a bath if the temperature is below 70 degrees unless there is an indoor wash rack with hot water. Even then, unless the horse is extremely sweaty and dirty, I try to avoid bathing by vacuuming. Vacuuming is usually effective in getting the horse clean if you start by going over the horse with a rubber curry comb. Use firm, circular strokes to loosen dirt and dry sweat. As I mentioned when discussing my daily grooming procedure, the vacuum cleaner not only removes that dirt and sweat, it also brings out the oil in the horse's skin for natural shine.

The tail is taken down from it's braid and washed. We apply a product which helps take out the tangles and gives the tail more shine. We then use a blow dryer to dry the tail while using our fingers to carefully separate each strand for maximum fullness.

The pleasure horse's mane is banded for several reasons. Banding creates a neater, cleaner appearance because the mane is held close to the horse's neck and is kept from moving about in the wind or with the horse's movement. It also makes the horse's neck look thinner and longer.

Just prior to the class, I oil the horse's hooves at most shows but at the really big events I use hoof black. I don't like to use it often, because it dries out a horse's foot. I use any of the commercial brands of "shine" products to grease the horse's muzzle, eyes and inside his ears. I also lightly spray on an oil-based product designed to make the haircoat and tail shine. Most importantly, I make sure I use adequate fly spray. I don't want to have wasted my time, training and entry fee because my horse went around the rail shaking his head or swishing his tail at flies.

MENTAL PREPARATION

Everybody prepares for competition in their own individual way. Personally, I try to follow the same routine way of doing things, whether it's going through and checking my horses while I feed them in the morning or spending plenty of time just sitting on the horse's back and relaxing while out in the arena, as I do at home every day.

I make a conscious effort to focus on positive things, and I don't allow myself to worry about what might happen. I know my horse and what I can expect of him. It's a waste of mental energy to fret about his weaknesses now. Furthermore, I'm a firm believer that if you think long and hard enough about what might go wrong, you just about guarantee that it will go wrong.

The closer I get to show time, the more I try to slow my pace down. I have a tendency to do things too fast or to make things happen rather than letting them happen once I get in the show pen. I try to keep myself from getting in this frame of mind before the class by taking my time with every little thing I do. It puts me in a slow motion frame of mind that is to my benefit once I'm in the pen. I'll be more likely to sit back and let things unfold naturally rather than rushing them along.

In the warm-up pen outside the arena, I spend the last few minutes before the class quietly warming up my horse by riding him pretty much the same way I do at home. I want him to be supple through the head and neck and responsive to my cues. I want him to be thinking about waiting on me. If he has a weakness, I drill him on it very subtly, but I usually don't get aggressive here because I don't have time to finish any wars I might start.

There are two things worth noting regarding the competition. It's very helpful to watch the horses you'll be showing against to rank them in your mind. That way when you go in the pen, you know which horses you want to be near and which ones you want to avoid. For example if you have a weak jogger, you want to follow another poor jogger. Or if you see a horse wringing his tail or pinning his ears, you want to avoid that horse altogether.

Do not, however, allow yourself to become "psyched out" by the competition. I often see people ride around in the warm-up pen watching the other riders. They see all kinds of new training methods and pretty soon they start trying them. They start thinking that all of the other horses look better than theirs and they panic. Do not allow this to happen. Stick to your program. It's what you know and what your horse knows. And at this point it's going to be far more effective than any new method you could try.

It also goes back to knowing your horse and what his potential is. I learned this the hard way while showing a reining horse a few years ago. It was a fairly major event, and I was sitting second after the first go-round. When I went back into the finals all I was thinking about was beating the first place horse. I over-rode my horse and ended up moving to tenth. Ironically the first place horse also had a bad ride, and the horse who was sitting third after the first go ended up winning. Afterward, a very wise and well-respected horseman named John Hoyt came up to me and pointed out my mistake. I'd pushed my horse past his limit, he said, whereas if I had only been satisfied with second place I would have won the whole deal. I've stuck to that theory ever since, and in the end I think it helps me win my fair share.

RESPONSIBILITIES ON THE RAIL

Once I'm in the class, I work hard at making everything look easy. This is done by incorporating all of the topics covered in this section. It requires the rider to really think and react, rather than just being a passenger.

My first priority is to concentrate on my horse's performance and how to cue, guide and aid him so that he rides his best. I know what the horse is capable of, and I go into the pen expecting that level of performance. Riders commonly make the mistake of expecting a horse to be perfect when they go into the pen, just because they think the horse has to be perfect in order to win. Be realistic. If your horse tends to miss the left lead at home, there's a good chance he'll miss it in the class. If the horse needs to be framed up about every ten strides at the jog while training him, know that you need to do the same when showing him. Knowing your horse is critical now that you're on the rail. Use what you've learned. For example, for the horse that misses the left lead, try to avoid loping off on that lead when the judge is looking directly at you. If you miss it, you may have another

If these horses continued jogging for just a stride or so longer, Doug would have to pass the black horse. However, the judge just called for the lope and the exhibitor on the black horse was wise enough to lope off immediately. By continuing at the jog for a moment before loping, Doug holds a good position on the rail.

chance before the judge sees your mistake. With the horse who needs a lot of help at the jog, try to position yourself near one or two other poor joggers. Your problems won't look so bad in comparison.

Remember also my earlier advice from the chapter on transitions, that a horse is more likely to stay good if he starts off good. Set your horse up properly for each of his transitions just as you would if you were riding at home. Novice riders in particular are prone to rush departures. If you normally ask your horse to lope off by picking up on your reins about an inch, gently laying your outside leg into his side and then "smooching," you will not get the same response if you just kick and "smooch" in the show pen. On the same note, many riders also suddenly become much heavier-handed once they get in an actual class. You don't jerk on your horse in training him, so don't jerk on him in the show pen. This is not how your horse was trained to slow down. It just scares him so he goes even faster.

In preparing your horse for competition, we discussed how to handle "traffic," or the other horses in the class, in Chapter 13. Follow those guidelines now that you're in the class. You checked out the competition before the class, now be aware of who's in front of, behind or beside you at all times. Try to maintain good rail position by looking for opportunities to get past or near the appropriate horses. Ideally, you'd like a major "hole," or a place all by yourself on the rail. But in the crowded classes that isn't possible. Therefore you have to look for an opportunity to cut across the corner of the pen or hold your horse back a little to create some space around you. Transitions and the reverse are often good for this. Cutting across the corner of a pen while passing can also help you get ahead of a horse you want behind you. Keep in mind, however, that you will be penalized for waiting more than a second or two to make your transitions or by doing anything else that common sense tells you is inconsiderate to other riders such as passing too closely.

It's also necessary to be very aware of where the judge or judges are and where their attention is focused. If possible, watch a pleasure class prior to your class to see where the judges stand and where they most often watch. Judges usually pick a certain area of the pen to concentrate on. When you're on the rail, use your peripheral vision, or what you can see without turning your head, to periodically check on the judge. This aids you in knowing whether to make an adjustment with your horse or not. I don't like an exhibitor to stare at the judge, but if your horse is riding particularly well and you don't think the judge has noticed, it's a good idea to make brief eye contact with a judge to help get your horse noticed. If you can look a judge in the eye with a pleasant expression on your face and then immediately return to looking forward down the rail, you express your confidence in your horse to the judge.

Corners are a good place to pass a slower horse.

If your horse is riding particularly well, as this one is, it's often a good idea to make brief eye contact with a judge to get his attention.

This pleasant expression is also part of a rider's body language, which is so important in western pleasure. No matter how well or how poorly your horse is riding, your facial expression and body's posture should be the same. It's a concept called "selling" your ride. This means the rider's posture and facial expression indicate that he's pleased with his horse and enjoying the ride. Since that's essentially what a pleasure class is all about, it's an important part of my role as the rider. Furthermore, if the rider looks like he is having a good ride, the judge is more likely to think the same. Always remember that western pleasure is largely based on a judge's opinion of your horse rather than hard, cold facts like whether you lost a cow or over spun.

A good showmen is always trying to influence the judge's opinion. If your horse truly is riding well, it accentuates this. If your horse has made a few mistakes, a confidant manner helps camouflage those mistakes or may even help lessen their consequences. This is not only true because the judge might be influenced into disregarding a slight error but also because it helps keep things from going from bad to worse. For example, let's say your horse stumbled while jogging right in front of the judge. If you react by keeping your balance in the saddle, subtly framing up your horse so he continues jogging and your facial expression never changes, the judge may penalize your horse slightly but he probably isn't going to disqualify you for it. There's even a chance he won't even notice the mistake. But if you react by immediately snapping your head around to look at the judge, grabbing your horse's face with your rein hand while leaning forward in the saddle, you've done two damaging things. Number one, you've made a mild error look like a huge mistake in the eyes of the judge. Secondly, you've scared your horse so that it takes even longer for him to recover and go back to working quietly.

This idea of keeping a positive expression on your face is just as important once the horses come off the rail and are lined up to demonstrate the back up. Perhaps even more so because the judge is close enough to really see your expression. At that point, you've just finished what you thought was a really great ride, a really terrible one or somewhere in between. But it's just your opinion of the ride, not the judge's. And it doesn't factor in how the other horses in the class rode. Therefore as the judge approaches to ask you to back your horse, I suggest keeping a positive, pleasant look on your face regardless of whether you think you won or lost. And remember that until his score card is turned in, the judge is still making up his mind. It's therefore not a good idea to keep pulling on your horse's head or moving him around in the line up.

17

Maintenance and Troubleshooting

For the purposes of this book, my definition of an older pleasure horse is any horse who is broke to show one-handed in a bridle. Once a pleasure horse reaches this point, he is ridden mostly for maintenance and to correct problems as they come along. The pleasure horse that is shown as a two-year-old will probably reach this point somewhere in his three-year-old year, so I touched on this topic near the end of Chapter 12, the last in the series of breaking and training chapters in this book. But since many readers started this book with an older horse, this chapter is designed for them.

There is not one, absolute answer as to which bit I ride an older horse in. It changes from day to day according to my goals and the preferences of the individual horses. I describe the main bits I use in Chapter 14, but beyond that let me add that it's a good idea to alternate between a bit with a solid mouthpiece and a snaffle so the horse does not get dull to one or the other.

I begin each riding session with the same suppling and bending exercises used for my younger horses. If the horse has never had this kind of riding I start off in a plain, ⅝-inch, smooth snaffle. I treat the horse just like a green broke two-year-old. If he's never been suppled, he's probably extremely stiff through the poll, neck and shoulder. It takes awhile for this horse to limber up.

I may also put the horse through a few of the serpentine and circle exercises described in Chapter 7. If it's new to him, it's good for him because it's a fresh approach to his training. I also long-trot and counter-canter the horse for endurance and coordination just as I did the younger horses. Most of the other ways I maintain a broke horse are purely for the mental aspect of the

horse's training. I don't ride the horse every day, unless I'm trying to get his energy level down just before a show. I ride in different environments, like out in the pasture, on the trails or even on the outside of my arena fence rather than on the inside. Sometimes even the simplest change can make a horse's world look completely different to him.

If the horse is not a problem horse, in other words he's relatively easy to maintain and he does not have a high energy level, I teach him to gallop large circles. I do this from the lope by leaning forward slightly in the saddle and moving my hand way up on his neck to urge him forward. I also use my outside leg to encourage the horse to gradually increase his speed. I make him move on like this for only two or three laps. To bring him back to a regular lope, I sit back in the saddle, push my weight down in the stirrups, and move my hand back to it's regular position. After loping for a lap or so, I stop him gently and let him settle. Teaching the horse to vary his speed like this is good for the horse mentally, but it has to be kept under control and should probably only be done on a limited basis with most pleasure horses.

Finally, another good way to keep a pleasure horse mentally fresh is to train him for other events. Personally I don't have a lot of time to spend doing this. But for the

(above) Doug often rides out in the pasture to keep an older horse fresh mentally.

(opposite) Doug supples the horse through the poll, neck and shoulder by working the horse in serpentine and circle exercises.

(pages 160-161) In reprimanding a horse for his mistakes, don't jerk on his mouth because that scares him. Pick up your hand to take the slack out of the reins and use both hands to shut the horse down.

In correcting a horse that "runs off" at the lope, Doug backs the horse up.

average amateur rider who keeps his or her horse at home, I strongly suggest teaching your horse to perform the necessary maneuvers for other classes like trail, horsemanship or western riding.

TROUBLESHOOTING

A pleasure horse is both smarter and lazier than we give him credit for. If his rider has a weakness, the horse will find it and use it. If he can find a way to "beat the system," he's going to do it. The following problems are typical of those an older pleasure horse might develop. Although these problems can be frustrating to the novice rider, there are usually relatively simple ways of correcting the problem. My suggestions for doing so should be used in conjunction with my regular program for riding an older pleasure horse. I also assume that your horse is broke to walk, jog and lope in both directions, as well as to back up and guide to a reasonable degree.

"RUNNING OFF"

If your horse consistently lopes too fast, you first have to determine whether you have a horse that tends to "run off" or one who just cannot lope slowly. As I've stated from the very beginning, every horse is not physically or mentally designed to be a pleasure horse. But if you know your horse can lope slowly, there are ways to help him do so. The simplest and most effective way I know to do this is by letting him make the mistake of speeding up and then stopping it.

Begin by asking the horse to lope. Sit back, put your hand down against his neck so that he has about the same amount of rein as you normally would in a pleasure class. Don't encourage the horse to go faster, but don't try to prevent it. As soon as he starts loping faster, pick up your hand to take the slack out of the reins and use both hands to shut the horse down. Do not say "whoa." Do not jerk the horse because that scares him. You want to have control of the horse's head, and then pull back as if to basically "sit" the horse down. If the horse is resistant, or it feels like he's pushing on your hands once you've stopped him, back him up a few steps to get him off your hands. Let him stand there and think about what has happened for a few seconds and then quietly lope him off again. Repeat this over and over in both directions. Sometimes, if a horse has a big problem with speed, I may do this 20 or 30 times a session for two or more weeks before the horse learns that he cannot "run off" at the lope. Again, the keys to success with this exercise are to let the horse make his mistake and to avoid jerking his mouth when stopping him.

"LISTENING" TO THE MICROPHONE OR ANTICIPATING THE GAITS

After they've been shown a lot and have learned the routine of a typical western pleasure class, many older horses start anticipating the next gait. Some even learn to change gaits when they hear the microphone click on rather than waiting on the rider to cue the horse. The best way, and perhaps the only way, to correct it is to use a few classes for schooling purposes. In other words, forget about winning a particular class and instead work on fixing your horse's problem. Before I explain how I do this, however, let me emphasize that the rider needs to use common sense and courtesy toward other exhibitors. Don't let your schooling session ruin someone else's good ride. You also might suggest that a local show offer a few practice classes for the purpose of schooling the horses in a real horse show environment.

The key to teaching a horse not to anticipate is to keep your cool. If you get mad and react by jerking your horse back when he starts to make his move, you only make the situation worse. Instead, when the horse anticipates, quietly and gently stop him. Be sure no one is directly behind you because you don't want to mess up their ride. Make the horse stand there while the other horses go past him. It's best if this is done on the rail, but it may be necessary for you to come off the rail and stand so you're not in the way. Don't jerk on the horse or try to get even in any way. It's punishment enough for the horse that he has to stand there while everyone else is moving. Once that particular gait is over with, put your horse back on the rail and continue with the class until he anticipates again. If he does, stop him and make him stand again. It's helpful if you can ride him in several classes in a row on that day. Eventually he starts thinking that maybe he does not know the routine after all.

"DULL-SIDED"

Many novice riders have trouble getting their horses into a lope. The simplest solution for this problem is to use one rein to reach back and lightly tap the horse on his hip or flank. I recommend, however, that a more experienced rider tries this first in case the horse bucks. If you cue the horse for the left lead, use the right rein to reach back and lightly tap the horse on the right flank. I prefer this method over spurring a horse because I think spurring tends to make a horse swish his tail. Tapping the horse with the rein usually makes a horse tuck his tail.

"SHYING"

First, I try to prevent a horse from shying during a class by getting him in the arena before I show and allowing plenty of time for him to see the sights. If your horse is truly scared of something in the arena, there are a couple of ways to approach the problem. The easiest way is to find another horse that is not afraid and make several passes in front of the obstacle following this horse. Once one horse sees that another is not afraid, he usually decides it's okay, too. If that doesn't work, I put the horse directly in front of whatever he's afraid of so he's facing the obstacle and aggressively "fence him" back in forth. This requires an experienced and strong rider who can pull the horse back and forth without letting him turn and run. It forces the horse to look at the obstacle. I also work the horse in small circles directly beside the obstacle at the walk, jog and lope so that he has to go by it over and over. Do not go all of the way around the pen because this allows too much time in between when the horse passes the obstacle.

"RUNNING OUT THE GATE"

This method also requires a good rider and some common sense. Do not use it if there are people, other horses or obstacles which might get in the way risking injury to a person or horse. Like my method of stopping a horse from running off, this one allows the horse to make his mistake and then punishes him for it. If my horse wants to duck out the gate as we ride by it, I let him go out the gate. Then I stop him, pick up the bridle reins with my off-hand and give him a light to medium crack across the flank. Then I walk him back into the arena, stop him on the rail and stand there. After a moment or two, I go back to working him on the rail. I trust him not to go out the gate as we pass it, and I do not try to prevent him from doing so. I'll probably have to repeat the exercise, quietly and patiently, two or three times but usually after about the third lesson he won't want to go out the gate. When I end the session, I get off the horse while in the arena and lead him out.

EAR PINNING AND BITING
OR KICKING AT OTHER HORSES

Unfortunately there's only so much you can do to stop a horse from pinning his ears once he's gotten a bad attitude. You can prevent it to some degree or at least minimize it by trying to keep the horse mentally fresh, but some horses just become old and grouchy like some people do. I also suggest having a veterinarian examine the horse to make sure he isn't lame or sore somewhere.

If your horse pins his ears, bites or kicks at other horses, he may never truly get over his dislike for other horses. But you can reprimand him for his actions, which will hopefully discourage him from showing his dislike for the other horses. Do this by finding someone to ride another quiet, broke horse along side you. Work on the rail as if you were in a class and wait on your horse to show his ill attitude. The moment he does, stop both horses, and give your horse one light to medium spanking with the end of the bridle reins across the flanks. The other horse should be standing right there. Allow your horse to settle for a moment, and then put both horses back to work on the rail. The moment your horse makes the mistake again, spank him again. The purpose is to show your horse that his threatening attitude did not make the other horse go away and that he will be punished if he pins his ears, kicks or bites.

18

Judging Western Pleasure

From the moment the gate is closed, the exhibitors in a western pleasure class are presenting their efforts at breeding or buying, training and now showing a pleasure horse. Each entry demonstrates the walk, jog and lope in both directions and then the back up. After studying the horses from the center of the pen, the judge places them according to his opinion of their performances.

A judge makes his decision based on the rules which govern the class combined with personal opinion. The latter is purely a matter of individual likes and dislikes and is unique to that particular judge. Personal opinion is also what makes western pleasure "anybody's ball game" each time the gate closes and the class begins.

Rules governing western pleasure classes are established by the various associations which either sponsor or sanction each show or futurity. People who want to show a western pleasure horse have many different levels of competition to choose from. Local saddle clubs and state-wide horse show associations sponsor "Open Shows" which are governed by each club's rules. In most any region of the country a person can find information about upcoming shows, usually held on Friday and Saturday evenings, in their local newspapers or posted on bulletin boards in area tack shops. Open shows are very popular, fun for riders of all ages, and affordable, with nominal entry fees that are usually less than fifteen dollars per class and none of the stall or hotel costs usually associated with major events.

Youth riders who wish to compete in western pleasure may want to consider their local 4-H horse program. Organized on a county level, in most areas 4-H offers a horse club which teaches young people about

WALK ▶▶▶

The walk is a four-beat gait with each leg moving independently, and with the hooves touching the ground at different times. According to NSBA rules, the walk should be "comfortable, flat and ground-covering." This gait is often the most indicative of the ideal pleasure horse's quiet, relaxed nature. It also lets the horses ease around the arena while the judges assess the overall attractiveness of each horse, including balance and conformation.

FIRST BEAT: Left back hoof strikes the ground.

JOG ▶▶▶

The jog is defined as "soft, relaxed and comfortable with a definite two-beat." The first beat occurs when the left hind and right front hooves hit the ground. The horse then lifts the opposite legs and swings them forward. The second beat is added when those two legs, the right hind and left front, strike the ground. Simply put, the horse is moving so that a hind foot and diagonal front foot hit the ground at precisely the same time. The speed and length of stride should be compatible with the horse's size.

FIRST BEAT: Left hind hoof and right front hoof strike the ground.

LOPE ▶▶▶

The three-beat lope begins when the rear drive hoof hits the ground. Next, the off-fore and leading hind hooves strike the ground almost simultaneously to make the second beat. The third beat is added when the lead hoof hits the ground. At the lope, the horse should provide the rider with a comfortable, natural, rolling motion, which is created by the horse's lift in the body and back. This graceful lift is what creates the slight hesitation between the first and second beats.

FIRST BEAT: Left hind hoof strikes the ground.

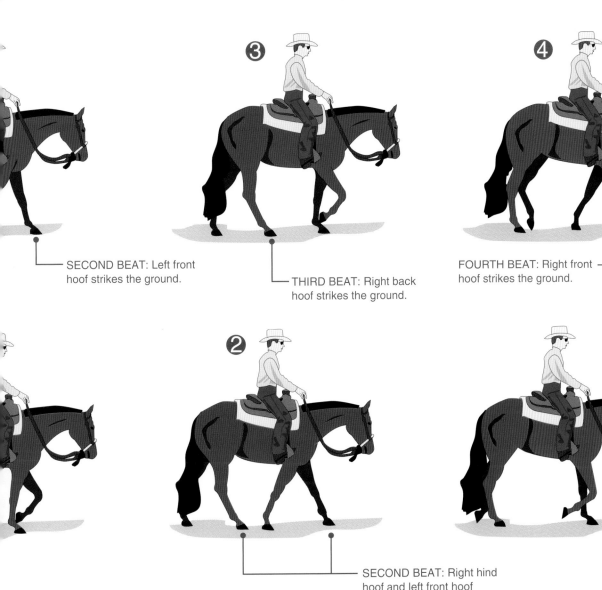

SECOND BEAT: Left front hoof strikes the ground.

THIRD BEAT: Right back hoof strikes the ground.

FOURTH BEAT: Right front hoof strikes the ground.

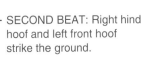

SECOND BEAT: Right hind hoof and left front hoof strike the ground.

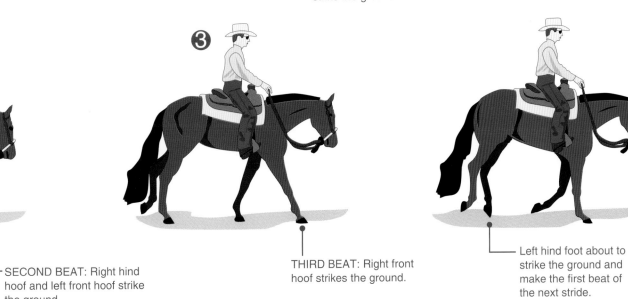

SECOND BEAT: Right hind hoof and left front hoof strike the ground.

THIRD BEAT: Right front hoof strikes the ground.

Left hind foot about to strike the ground and make the first beat of the next stride.

many different aspects of horsemanship. These clubs offer members an opportunity to participate in local fun shows as well as state and regional competitions. For further information, contact the County Extension Service listed in your local phone directory.

Various breed organizations, including those for registered Quarter Horses, Paints, Appaloosas and Palominos, sanction shows which are often held over a two or more day schedule known as a circuit. A separate show usually takes place on each day, with a different judge or judges for each day. A few extremely large single breed shows, such as the All American Quarter Horse Congress, are spread out over several days or even weeks. Show dates and detailed information about the shows are published in the associations' official publications. Additionally, each association has one or more national event in which exhibitors compete for prestigious world championship titles.

The governing body for most western pleasure futurities is the National Snaffle Bit Association. Futurities are competitions in which exhibitors usually compete for large cash prizes and the classes are divided by the horse's age, for example the Two-Year-Old Snaffle Bit Western Pleasure. Futurity events also offer classes for horses over the age of three, known as maturities, as well as hunter under saddle and longe line events. Each futurity is sponsored by a different organization across the country and is usually held over a two or three day period, sometimes in conjunction with a regular breed show. NSBA unifies the industry by establishing standard rules which define what is both favorable and unfavorable as well as by providing a judging system which educates and governs the men and women who pick the winners. Futurities which are sanctioned by NSBA must abide by NSBA rules regarding judging, distribution of prize money, tack and equipment, etc. Exhibitors, who must be NSBA members, are thereby assured that when they attend a NSBA futurity they will be judged by a familiar and acceptable set of rules. Many other associations also base their rules on NSBA regulations.

Nearly all associations, including NSBA and those which sanction open shows and registered events, offer a means of rewarding success by providing a points system. Points are tabulated in two ways; either yearly or for a horse's lifetime. Many saddle clubs which sponsor open shows, nearly all breed associations and NSBA award points to horses and or riders for winning or placing in their events. At the end of the year, high point winners are rewarded with prizes which may range from a trophy or belt buckle to a saddle or even a horse trailer. Many times the competition for these year end titles and awards is fierce. In the AQHA, for example, the high point title is known as the "Honor Roll," and some exhibitors spend an entire year hauling across the country to shows which they have thoughtfully chosen according to the number of points they are likely to acquire there.

Points which are awarded to horses on a lifetime basis are generally tabulated by breed associations. Horses earn these points in the same manner as they do yearly points, by winning or placing in events sanctioned by the particular association. By earning certain numbers of points, horses achieve recognition titles. For example, in the AQHA, a "Register of Merit" is awarded to a horse which earns ten points in the open division or an amateur or youth with any one horse in their respective division which has won at least ten points in one or more events. AQHA also offers a Superior Award, a Supreme Championship and other titles which are intended to recognize the outstanding achievements of registered Quarter Horses. Besides being "bragging rights" for the horse's owner, titles also increase the horse's value.

This chapter is designed to familiarize the reader with the standard rules which govern NSBA western pleasure classes. NSBA rules were chosen because they are highly detailed, have remained fairly consistent over time and are considered to be standard within the industry. For those readers who compete in events sanctioned by breed associations, please contact that association for an updated rule book. Addresses are included in the Appendix. All information in quotes is taken directly from the NSBA Handbook. It is printed with permission from NSBA, but is not intended to take the place of the association's official handbook. Please refer to the current NSBA Handbook for up-to-date information as rules may change from year to year.

Before covering the specifics by which western pleasure is judged, consider the purpose and goals of the NSBA event which are defined as follows:

"To train and develop all horses in a humane manner, protecting at all times, their physical and mental potentialities.

"To promote kinder training methods, resulting in a more efficient horse.

"To establish a greater market for good pleasure horses - horses that have soft mouths, respond to a light rein and have a comfortable head carriage."

REQUIRED GAITS

Walk "The walk should be comfortable, flat and ground-covering."

Jog "The jog should be soft, relaxed and comfortable with a definite two beat. At no time would it resemble a running walk nor should it be rough and stilted. The speed and stride should be compatible with the horse's size."

Lope "The lope should be soft, rolling and comfortable with strong emphasis on a natural three beat."

Back up "Horses should back, on command, quietly, willingly and easily on a straight line without resistance. Jawing, resisting or tossing head to be penalized."

JUDGING

Horses must be sound of sight, wind and limb. All horses will be judged as a pleasure horse at the walk, jog, lope and back as well as on all transitions between gaits. Horses must work both ways of the ring at three gaits. Horse must reverse to the inside (away from the rail). They may be required to reverse at the walk or jog, at the discretion of the judge, but shall not be asked to reverse at the lope.

A pleasure horse should be a happy horse and a natural horse. Emphasis is to be placed on good movers, manner and attitude as reflected in the horse's ears, mouth, tail and way of going. Judges are instructed to pay particular attention to the above mentioned and any attempt to alter the above is to be severely penalized.

In two-year-old or three-year-old snaffle bit events, all entries must be shown with both hands on reins, maintaining light contact with the horse's mouth. The rider's hands should be carried near the pommel and not further than four inches out on either side of the saddle horn. A tight rein or excessive slack is at no time acceptable. Head carriage should be quiet and comfortable. Horses are to be severely penalized for carrying their heads consistently behind the vertical in their gaits.

If a horse's mouth shows signs of broken skin, rawness or bleeding the horse will be eliminated from competition. If a horse's nose or any area touched by the bosal shows signs of broken skin, rawness or bleeding the horse will be eliminated from competition. Prior to the judge's final placing, he must inspect the noses or mouths of the horses in the finals line for raw or abused areas.

FAULTS

Faults of the horse and rider are penalized as follows:

A) Missed lead or break of gait, for up to two strides, shall be penalized at least three placings.

B) Missed lead or break of gait, for three or more strides, shall be penalized by not placing or by placing last in small classes.

C) Any loss of forward motion during transitions shall be penalized up to three places on judges' card.

D) Refusal to back must be penalized a minimum of three places on judges' card.

EQUIPMENT

Two-Year-Old and Three-Year-Old Snaffle Bit Events

The only difference between equipment rules for two-year-olds versus the three-year-olds is that the former are ineligible for competition if they have previously been shown in anything other than a snaffle bit or bosal. Three-year-olds are not restricted as to type of equipment used while ridden in other classes.

Snaffle Bit - must be smooth snaffles, i.e. broken mouthpieces, with ring no larger than four inches and no smaller than two inches; from the cheek to one inch in from the cheek must be a minimum ⅜ inch in diameter with a gradual decrease to the center of the snaffle; curb straps are optional, but if used must be leather or nylon only and must be attached below the reins.

Bosal or Hackamore - must be braided rawhide or leather, no more than three-quarter inch in diameter at the cheek; must be a minimum of one-finger space (approximately ¾ inch) between the bosal and nose; no metal under the jaw or on the noseband in connection with the bosal.

Maturity Western Pleasure

The Maturity events are opened to three-year-old and older horses. Horses may be ridden in standard western bits as approved by AQHA or in a snaffle bit or bosal as described above.

19

It's Been A Pleasure

KRISTY IMAGE

By Triple's Image and out of Little Brown Jag, Kristy Image was one of the first really outstanding pleasure horse I rode and showed. She was a big, brown mare with a long neck and a lot of shape to her, and she was one of those unique horses that caught everybody's eye.

She first got my attention while Tommy Manion and I were at the Florida Gold Coast back when I worked for him. A young girl named Nicole Sawyer from Oklahoma City had the mare there. We couldn't keep our eyes off the mare because she was such a good mover and had so much presence about her. After a couple of days, Nicole came to us and asked for help riding the mare. From the first time I rode her, we hit it off and Nicole sent her to us for training.

Kristy Image helped me realize how rewarding it can be to ride pleasure horses. I got along good with the mare and the mare got along with me. She was a fickle mare, and you could wind her clock up real easy, so I had to spend a lot of time with her. But it was time that I enjoyed because she was both talented and smart. I learned to work on her real easy, letting her come at her own pace, and it paid off. In 1980 I won a major futurity in Kansas City and she went on to win two classes at the Congress with Tommy as well as a World Championship in Junior Western Pleasure. After her show career, she made an outstanding broodmare.

MISS DOCS MELODY

This mare was not only a great pleasure horse, she also taught me many valuable lessons back when I first got started as a horse trainer. I liked her because she

AMERICAN
PAINT HORSE
WORLD
CHAMPIONSHIPS

LEXINGTON

Paint Me Zippo

CHAMPION

Don Shugart

had natural ability, yet she also had a fire inside her that made it a challenge to prepare her to show. By Doc's Melody and out of a mare named Stark V Bar, she was owned and shown in Amateur events by Karen Sullivant of Aubrey, Texas. We both won a World Championship on her in 1981.

Miss Docs Melody's best gear was definitely the lope. She was an adequate jogger, but she could really lope. Not only was she very good behind, she was also super flat up front. She could lope slow, but most importantly she had a lot of feel or rhythm as most of the great horses do.

The tricky part to riding this mare was her mind. She was hot-blooded and in training her I soon learned that I had to take my time and be patient if I wanted to keep her moving slow. If I let her frustrate me and I pushed her past her limit, she could turn a fight into war. Once I figured that out, I found that I really liked the challenge of keeping a horse contained mentally while teaching them how to do things my way. Many of the horses I have been successful with in my career have had this type of personality, and I credit Miss Docs Melody with teaching me how to properly prepare a hot-blooded horse.

HOTRODDERS JET SET

Hotrodders Jet Set is one of my all-time favorite horses and certainly the most athletic pleasure horse I have ever ridden. Keith Whistle and I purchased half of the 1979 bay stallion after we first saw him as an unbroke two-year-old at Elwin Rainwater's place in California. I started riding him the following January, and the first weekend in March we won two six point junior western pleasure classes. He was the easiest horse I have ever trained because he was so talented he practically trained himself.

Besides being exceptionally light in the mouth and really smart, Hotrodders Jet Set had amazing athletic ability. You could rope cattle on him, change leads or do whatever you wanted to with him. He was one of those unique individuals that every single time I rode him he got better and better. I always said I could ride him in a halter and he'd just keep improving. Needless to say, he was a whole lot of fun to ride.

Owned by Tom and Carrie Chown of Pilot Point, Texas, when he died in 1992 following a freak breeding accident, Hotrodders Jet Set left his mark not only on my career but also on the pleasure horse industry. He had points in halter and western pleasure and was the AQHA High Point Western Riding Stallion in 1985. He sired 348 total get who have earned over 5,000 points in 13 events, and in 1993, Hotrodders Jet Set was inducted into the NSBA Hall of Fame.

MS MBJ MUDLARK

This bay mare by Mr Impressive and out of Mrs Ranchero Step was one of those legendary, once in a lifetime show horses that trainer's dream of. She only lived to be a six-year-old, but in that short time she stole a lot of horsemen's hearts, including mine. Mudlark was breath-taking to look at, even if she was just standing

(pages 176-177) I won two APHA World Championships on Paint Me Zippo, a talented, attractive Paint stallion by Zippo Pine Bar.

(opposite top) Kristy Image was one of those big, striking horses that caught everybody's eye. Riding her helped me realize how rewarding it is to train pleasure horses.

(opposite bottom) I credit Miss Docs Melody, the mare I won a World Championship with in 1981, with teaching me how to ride a hot-blooded horse.

Hotrodders Jet Set was an exceptionally talented athlete and a whole lot of fun to ride.

The ultimate show horse, Ms MBJ Mudlark was a true pleasure to ride. I was reserve with her at the Texas Classic and the All American Quarter Horse Congress when she was a two-year-old, and then we came back and won the Congress Three-Year-Old Pleasure Derby in 1985.

still, and she was such an elegant mover that the picture was even prettier when she was on the rail. Originally owned by John Mulholland, whom I worked for in Oklahoma, he sold her to Chris Barlow of Connecticut who owned her until the mare died in her stall from unknown causes.

What I most enjoyed about her was that she was the ultimate show horse. She was really easy-going, almost lazy or disinterested when I rode her at home. She'd convince me that she couldn't win anything she was so sloppy and flat. Then when I went into the pen she'd turn on the charm. It was almost like she knew that when we cleaned her up and the judges and crowd were all watching, it was time to go to work. She showed great. Then, when you walked out the gait, she went back to being her old, lazy self and you just about had to drag her back to the stall. Mudlark placed second at the Texas Classic, the Grand Twenty and the Congress as a two-year-old. She won the Congress Three-Year-Old Pleasure Derby in 1985. I also won the World Championship in Junior Western Riding with her in 1986.

RACY RUMORS

I had a ball with Racy Rumors. She had so much expression and such a unique way of handling herself in different situations. To a lot of people, she would have just been a big pain. And she was difficult. But to me she was also a lot of fun because it was always a challenge to get her prepared and shown, without her throwing a fit. Sometimes she threw a fit. But that was just the way she was, and I had to accept it and try to work around it if I wanted to show her. She was such a great mover, it was worth it.

Racy absolutely hated a lot of commotion, so it was really hard to prepare her, especially at the Congress. She didn't like being around a lot of horses or people and she absolutely despised the overhang where everybody warms up at the Congress. To prepare her to be shown there, I came up with a system - kind of like a relay team of communications - whereby I could warm her up away from that area, but still get her in the pen in time to show. So while everybody else was riding under the overhang, I was on the mare way out in the infield riding all by myself. There weren't any loudspeakers out there so I didn't know what was going on in the show pen. Keith Whistle was showing her, and he was stationed by the gate into the coliseum. My wife, Tammy, positioned herself in between Keith and me. Just minutes before Keith had to ride into the class, he signaled to Tammy who then signaled to me. I jogged the mare straight to the gate and jumped off. Keith immediately jumped on and went right in the show pen. It worked and Racy won the Congress Junior Western Pleasure as a two-year-old.

Racy was a mare that had to be shown fresh, because if she was tired she wouldn't hold herself up and tended to move on too much. At the same time, she had an engine inside of her and it seemed that she could wind herself up. And once you got her wound up, you might as well take her back to the stall because there was no unwinding her. You couldn't lope her down, and you couldn't longe it out of her. In order for Racy to ride her best, I had to keep her contained mentally, and I really had to be careful. Still, all that made preparing her a challenge as well as very rewarding when she won.

Owned by the Rollins Brown of Florida as a young mare, she was later sold to Chris and Holly LaLonde of Canal Winchester, Ohio, where she is now proving herself as a broodmare. Racy is by Mr Conclusion and out of Brinks Bars Ginger.

PAINT ME ZIPPO

I broke this handsome Paint stallion by Zippo Pine Bar and out of Blazer Bonanza for Larry Ward of Tupelo, Mississippi, and sold him as a two-year-old to Yarnelle Farms of Fort Wayne, Indiana. He was an interesting horse because he was very broncy as a green colt. I could ride him for twenty or thirty minutes and then all of a sudden he might break in half and try to buck me off. I loved the challenge, but it was a little unnerving not knowing when you might land in the dirt! Eventually he outgrew it, and he became one of the most fun horses I've ever shown. He was very, very steady in the show pen. There were many times I honestly think I could have taken off the bridle in the middle of the class and he would have never missed a beat.

That steadiness paid off and in 1989 I won the Two-Year-Old Snaffle Bit Futurity at the APHA National Championship Show. In 1991, I came back to the World Show with Paint Me Zippo and won the Junior Western Pleasure under all five judges.

TNT FLUID FRED

TNT Fluid Fred was another stallion who is among my favorites not only for his talent but also for his attitude. His sire is Docs Bo Acres and his dam is Rascals Satin Doll. Keith and I bought him for a friend and good client, Ken Tugwell of Amite, Louisiana, at the Tom Powers Futurity in 1991. We won the Junior Pleasure at the Congress with him as well as the World Championship in Two-Year-Old Snaffle Bit Western Pleasure that year.

A very talented stallion, Fred didn't take a lot of training. He was the kind of horse you could just kind of lope the fresh off of and then show him. He didn't require a lot of preparation or my ingenuity either mentally or physically. Furthermore, if I made a mistake in training or pushed too hard, he was the kind of horse that didn't hold a grudge. I could get off him and go drink a coffee and when I got back on he would have forgotten about whatever argument we might have had. He was a very forgiving show horse, that now stands at stud for owners Chris and Holly LaLonde.

Preparing Racy Rumors to show was always a challenge, however it made her many wins especially rewarding.

Keith Whistle and I won both the Congress Junior Western Pleasure and the Two-Year-Old Snaffle Bit Western Pleasure at the AQHA World Show in 1991 with TNT Fluid Fred. The bay stallion is one of the most forgiving, easy-going stallions I've ever trained.

181

Glossary

All American Quarter Horse Congress—termed the world's largest horse show. An annual Quarter Horse show held in October at the fairgrounds in Columbus, Ohio. The Congress is organized by the Ohio Quarter Horse Association.

American Quarter Horse Association(AQHA)—breed organization responsible for registering Quarter Horses, recording the sale and transfer of Quarter Horses, monitoring activities in which Quarter Horses are involved and approving shows and races.

Animated—an undesirable way of moving in which the horse uses too much knee and hock action.

AQHA World Championship Show—annual competition for Quarter Horses which have qualified throughout the year in AQHA approved shows. Horses with the specified number of points are eligible to compete against other qualified horses to determine the world champions in each event. The World Show takes place in Oklahoma City, Oklahoma, each November.

Balance—a desirable quality in regard to a horse's conformation in which the front half of the body and the back half match. A well-balanced horse has a short back, a long underline, matching shoulder and hip angles and his neck is of a length that is proportionate to the rest of his body.

Bell boots—protective boots that cover the horse's coronary band.

Bosal—thick nosepiece made of braided leather; part of a hackamore bridle.

Bridled—horse that is flexed at the poll in response to the bit so that his face is vertical or past vertical with the ground.

Broke—describes a well-trained horse.

Broodmare—a female horse used for breeding purposes.

Cadence—each stride a horse takes is exactly the same distance as the rest.

Capture—a slang term meaning control of the horse's head and neck by the rider.

Cantle—the rear of the seat of the saddle.

Cavesson—leather noseband that helps prevent the horse from opening his mouth.

Chin strap—also called "curb strap." A leather strap that attaches to the cheek pieces of the bit. It fits under the horse's jawbone and works in conjunction with a bit to exert leverage on the horse's mouth. There are also "curb chains," which are made of metal links, that lie flat against the horse's jawbone.

Cinch—the strap around the horse's belly that holds the saddle on the horse's back. Also called the "girth."

Clean—describes a horse's legs that are free from scars or disfigurements which might indicate lameness. Also describes a neck that is not thick or meaty looking.

Collected—describes a horse that moves with sufficient drive from the hind legs and proper reach with the front legs at the jog or the lope.

Cold-backed—describes a horse that is inclined to buck when first saddled.

Colt—a male horse under the age of four.

Conformation—the general shape and size of a horse, the way in which a horse's body is put together.

Counter-canter—the horse lopes a circle on the wrong lead. For example, the horse lopes a right circle on the left lead.

Dam—female parent of a horse.

Direct rein—direct pressure from a pull on the reins: i.e. horse responds to a tug on the right rein by turning right in the direction of the direct pull.

Downhill—a term used regarding conformation that describes a horse whose hip is much higher than his wither. Also used to describe a horse that carries its head and neck excessively low, either due to conformation or the training the horse has been subjected to.

Drive from behind—see "impulsion."

Expression—the attitude a horse or rider conveys to the judge.

Filly—a female horse under the age of four. As she matures, she is referred to as a mare.

Finished—a horse that has successfully completed a training program and is considered well-broke.

Flat-kneed—a horse that moves with minimal bend at the knee is described as "flat-kneed."

Flexing at the poll—phrase used to describe when a horse tips his head down, making it approximately perpendicular to the ground. A horse flexes at the poll when the rider exerts pressure on the bit to bring the head into line.

Framed up—describes a horse that is carrying his head so that his poll is almost level with his withers and his face is close to perpendicular with the ground.

Futurity—a competition in which the classes are divided by the horse's age, for example Two-Year-Old Snaffle Bit Western Pleasure. Classes for two and three-year-olds are considered futurity classes, and the horses are normally shown in snaffle bits or bosals. Futurities also offer classes for older horses (see "Maturities") as well as hunter under saddle and longe line classes.

Gelding—a castrated male horse.

Girth—see "cinch."

Green—a horse that is barely broke is said to be "green."

Ground tie—a training technique in which the horse is taught to stand quietly without being physically tied to anything. The handler simply drops the lead rope or reins and tells the horse "whoa." The horse responds by standing still.

Hackamore—a bitless bridle of Spanish origin consisting of a headstall, bosal or rawhide noseband, heel knot and hair ropes (mecate) used as reins. Pressure points used to control the horse are the nose and jaw.

Headstall—leather strap that goes around the top of the horse's head to secure the bit.

Hollows out—phrase used to describe a horse that drops his back and does not adequately drive with the rear legs at the jog or lope. The horse also frequently raises his head and neck which creates an undesirable, "strung out" appearance.

Impulsion—the function of the hind legs at the jog and the lope. The hind legs reach under the horse's body and provide forward momentum, as well as a balancing point as the horse reaches forward with the front legs. The further the horse places his hind legs under his body, the greater the "impulsion."

Indirect rein—also called "neck rein." The horse is guided by pressure on his neck instead of his mouth, as in direct rein. When rein is placed on horse's neck, he moves in the opposite direction.

Jointed mouthpiece—also called "broken mouthpiece." Mouthpiece of a bit is jointed in the middle, often associated with snaffle bits.

Knee—describes the amount of bend a horse has in its front legs, particularly at the lope.

Leads—a horse is said to be on the right or left lead depending upon which front leg is leading in a lope. For example, in a right lead, the horse's right foreleg strides forward farther than does the left foreleg.

Light-sided—describes a horse that is sensitive or responsive to a rider's legs.

Longe—a means of exercising a horse in which the horse is worked in a small circle (approximately 40 to 60 feet in diameter) on a longe line or turned loose in a round pen. Horse is maneuvered around the pen by the use of body language, voice cues and or a longing whip.

Mare—a female horse over the age of four.

Maturity—a western pleasure class designed for three-year-old and older horses. Entries are normally shown one-handed in a bridle, as opposed to two-handed in a snaffle bit or bosal. Maturity classes are held at futurity events.

Mouthing the bit—an undesirable chewing or opening of the mouth that indicates the horse dislikes the bit.

National Snaffle Bit Association(NSBA)—organization dedicated to the activities of western pleasure and hunter under saddle horses. It approves shows, establishes rules by which the shows are governed, and guidelines regarding how the horses are to be judged.

Neck rein—see "indirect rein."

Packing the bridle—phrase used to describe a horse that responds to the bit by holding his head and neck in the proper position, i.e. with his poll close to level with his withers and his face almost perpendicular with the ground.

Palate—roof of the horse's mouth.

Poll—the area of the horse's head located between the ears. Joins the skull with the spinal cord of the neck.

Port—the upward curve of the mouthpiece in the center of a curb bit. Ports can be called "high" or "low" depending on the degree of the curve.

Profile—the side view of a horse.

Prospect—a horse, which by its breeding, conformation, disposition and way of moving, appears to be suited for a particular event.

Rollback—a stationary turn on the haunches. A 180 degree turn on the hocks accomplished when a horse stops, pivots on inside hind leg and moves off in other direction.

Running martingale—equipment which regulates head carriage. Consists of straps that attach to the girth, either under the horse's belly or at horse's sides under stirrup fenders. Divided into two branches, each with a ring at the end through which the reins pass. It prevents a horse from raising his head past a certain point.

Sacking out—rubbing the horse's entire body with a cloth, blanket, sack or some object. A desensitizing process used most often on a spooky or young horse in order to get the animal over the fear of being handled or of particular objects.

Shank—the long cheek pieces of a bit. Shank bits are to be used with chin or curb straps and allow the rider to exert leverage on a horse.

Sidepass—lateral movement at the walk, i.e. the horse moves directly left or right rather than forward or backward.

Side-pull—a soft, thin rawhide noseband with rings on the sides to attach reins and a soft rope chin strap.

Sire—male parent of a horse.

Slow-legged—phrase used to describe a horse that moves at the relaxed pace considered desirable in a pleasure horse. A "slow-legged" horse leaves his feet on the ground for a maximum amount of time while still performing the required number of beats of the walk, jog or lope.

Snaffle bit—a bit with a jointed or broken mouthpiece. The absence of shanks means that the rider pulls directly on the horse's mouth.

Sound—describes a horse which is not lame.

Splint boots—protective boots which cover the horse's front cannon bones.

Spurs—metal devices that attach to the heels of riding boots. They have shanks with a blunt point or rowels which poke into the horse to encourage movement. Accentuate rider's leg aids.

Staying back—phrase used to describe a horse that chooses to move at a relaxed pace as opposed to one that surges forward if not restrained by the rider.

Stallion—a male horse over the age of four that has not been castrated.

Stirrup fenders—connect the stirrups with the saddle under the rider's thigh.

Supple—to soften or make flexible the horse's body parts through various exercises.

Surcingle—a bitting rig used to teach the horse where to carry his head. Consists of a wide leather girth that reaches all the way around a horse's belly and back. It has several rings that are positioned along the horse's sides and back to which the reins are attached.

Throat latch—the point where the horse's head and neck are joined.

Topline—the side view of the horse's poll, neck, withers, back and across the top of his hindquarters.

Traffic—the other horses in a western pleasure class.

Wander—a slang term meaning the horse veers off in a direction other than the one the rider intended.

Weanling—a horse, of either sex, from weaning to one-year-old.

Wolf teeth—small teeth that have no function in a horse's mouth. They develop in front of a horse's molars. Pulling them is usually a simple operation and prevents a horse from injuring himself when there is a bit in his mouth.

Yearling—a horse, of either sex, from January 1 of the year after he was foaled until January 1 of the next year, at which time he is considered a two-year-old.

Appendix A: Association Addresses

American Paint Horse Association
P.O. Box 961023
Fort Worth, TX 76161-0023
phone (817) 439-3400

American Quarter Horse Association
P.O. Box 200
Amarillo, TX 79168
phone (806) 376-4811

Appaloosa Horse Club, Inc.
P.O. Box 8403
Moscow, ID 83843-0903
phone (208) 882-5578

National Snaffle Bit Association
One Indiana Square
Suite 2540
Indianapolis, IN 46204
phone (317) 632-6722

Palomino Horse Breeders of America
15253 E. Skelly Drive
Tulsa, OK 74116-2637
phone (918) 438-1234

Index

Acknowledgements

I sincerely thank the following people and organizations for their help in the preparation of this book. The **American Quarter Horse Association**, including Quarter Horse Journal editor **Jim Jennings**, for assistance with the chapters on the evolution of western pleasure, breeding and judging. **Dale Livingston** and **Jody Galyean**, renowned pleasure horse trainers, for their help and recollections regarding the evolution of western pleasure. **Danny Terry**, farrier, for all the information regarding tips on shoeing pleasure horses. **Kathy Kadash**, editor of Reining: The Art of Performance in Horses, for her support and advice which was of enormous value to me in creating both the manuscript and the photography for this book. The **National Snaffle Bit Association**, an organization dedicated to the promotion of pleasure horses, for its cooperation and permission to reprint part of the NSBA Handbook. The people who graciously allowed me to photograph pleasure horses on location at their barns and ranches: **Troy and Vickie Oakley**, **Dale Livingston**, **Jerry and Danelle Griffin**, **Donna Morgan**, **Edgewood Farms** and **Kiff Parrish**.

Carolyn S. Pryor

Photo Credits

With the exception of the following pages, all pictures in this book, including front and back covers, were photographed by Carolyn S. Pryor.

Preface, Reggie Bulger

Profile
12	Jacqueline Carpenter
13	Harold Campton Photography

Chapter 1
17-18	Ben Meriweather
20	Potter Photography
21	Harold Campton Photography
22	Harold Campton Photography

Chapter 2
26	(Speedy Glow) Jim Villas
26	(The Invester) Dalco Photography
27	Peri Photography

Chapter 16
150-151	Harold Campton Photography

Chapter 19
176-177	Don Shugart Photography
178	(Miss Docs Melody) Quarter Horse Journal
179	Don Shugart Photography
180	Don Shugart Photography
181	(Racy Rumors) Rick Childress
181	(TNT Fluid Fred) Harold Campton Photography

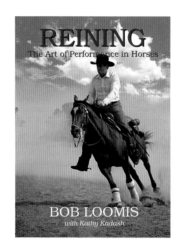
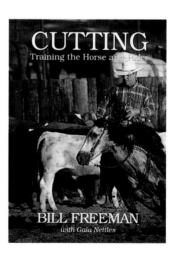